Barbara James is a writer who specialises in environmental education and animal issues. Her books include *Waste and Recycling* (1989), *Conserving the Polar Regions* (1990), and *This Fragile Earth* (1991) and *World Resources* (1991) both with John Baines. She lives in Hertfordshire.

D0715567

THE
YOUNG PERSON'S
ACTION GUIDE TO
ANIMAL RIGHTS

Barbara James

With illustrations by
Sarah-Jayne Stafford

The Author and Publisher wish to thank the following for their
permission to reproduce the quotations in this book:

page xvii *The Animal Contract* © Desmond Morris published by
Virgin Publishing April 1990; page 9 *The Tale of Little Pig Robinson*
by Beatrix Potter, 1987 edition. Reproduced by permission of
Frederick Warne & Co., page 83 Dr John Webster, Department of
Animal Husbandry, University of Bristol; page 100 *Animals in
Research* by D. Sperlinger 1981. Reprinted by permission of John
Wiley & Sons, Ltd.; page 112 The author has been unable to trace
the original source of this quotation; page 113 *Towards Animal Rights*
© Martyn Ford published by Animal Aid 1984.

Published by VIRAGO PRESS Limited 1992
20–23 Mandela Street, Camden Town, London NW1 0HQ

A CIP catalogue record for this title
is available from the British Library

Printed in Great Britain by
Cox & Wyman Ltd, Reading, Berkshire

ACKNOWLEDGEMENTS

I should like to thank the many organisations who provided me with information particularly Animal Aid, the Research Defence Society, the Royal Society for the Prevention of Cruelty to Animals and the Royal Society for the Protection of Birds.

Many thanks must also go to John Callaghan, Deputy Head of Education at the RSPCA and Lisbeth Grundy for reading the manuscript and making many helpful suggestions. Also, to John Baines who not only read and commented on the manuscript but also provided tea, encouragement and support when needed.

CONTENTS

Preface

Each year millions of animals are battered, blinded, addicted to drugs, mutilated and eventually killed in experiments performed by humans. Countless others perish in abattoirs, traps, nets, by guns, dogs and by neglect. Whole communities are wiped out when their habitats are destroyed. The horror story of animal suffering seems endless.

Animals are powerless in the face of human domination of the planet. They cannot speak for themselves or fight back. But they have one ally – people who care about their plight and want a better deal for animals.

Pressure for change often comes from you. You can be very effective in challenging and influencing decision-makers. Remember politicians want your vote, banks and shops want your money and the media want your attention. You can communicate what *you* want from *them* through what you say, buy or do. You can also influence people closer to home. Research has shown that many adults now buy free-range eggs or cruelty-free cosmetics because their children have educated them about animal welfare!

But bringing about change on important issues has never been easy. Those people who sought to abolish slavery, introduce votes for women or, more recently, protect the environment all faced tremendous inertia and opposition. You need a lot of courage, tenacity and patience to take a stand against long-established opinions and habits, especially when some older people dismiss young people's views as idealistic and naive. There is no reason to assume that campaigning for the proper treatment of animals will be any easier, but maybe in twenty years' time we will look back and wonder why there was any argument. Who today would consider reintroducing slavery or taking away votes for women?

This book is a guide to the animal rights and animal welfare issues in our society. It looks at the practical and moral issues, and it also gives you ideas for action. But it is only a starting point. It's up to you to make the changes happen. Animals don't have a voice, but you do. You can use it.

Where do you stand?

Below are some questions to get you thinking. This is not a quiz, and there are no right or wrong answers. Try to answer the questions honestly and take some time to think about your answers, rather than just saying 'yes' or 'no'. Try the questions before you read the book and again afterwards. See if you have changed any of your opinions. You can answer them on your own, with friends or family, or take them to a discussion group or club.

1. List, in order, your five favourite animals and your five least favourite. Would you treat your five favourites differently from your least favourite?

2. What is your fondest memory of an animal? What is your worst?

3. You are told you have to make one of the following animal species extinct. Which would you choose:
a) armadillo?
b) earthworm?
c) giant panda?
d) humans?
e) robin?
f) Atlantic salmon?

4. Would you be willing to take a new medicine if it had not been tested on animals first?

5. Is it all right to take animals from the wild to:
a) perform in a circus?
b) advertise petrol?
c) use them in cancer research?
d) put them in captive breeding programmes to save their species?
e) use them in zoo education programmes?
f) cook and eat them?

Ask yourself these questions again – first, if the animal was a chimpanzee and second, if it was a fish.

6. You see a person wearing a sealskin coat. How would you react? Would you say anything? Would you feel differently if the person was a Native North American in the Arctic or a business-person in a smart London hotel?

What if the person is wearing a leather coat?

7. You find a badly injured bird. Would you be able to kill it to put it out of its misery?

8. Would you be willing to kill an animal yourself to eat it? What if you were starving?

In some countries it is acceptable to eat cats or grasshoppers, while in others eating cows or pigs is forbidden. Which animals are you prepared to eat? Do you know why?

9. You are in the supermarket and see on the shelf two identical shampoos. One has a 'not tested on animals' label but costs 50p more than the other bottle. Which would you buy?

Would you be prepared to leave a shop and go to another one if they didn't sell cruelty-free products?

You go to the hairdresser's and have your hair washed. Would you ask the hairdresser if the shampoo was tested on animals?

10. Do you think people who are cruel to animals are more likely to be cruel to humans?

11. For £1,000 would you be prepared to kill
a) an ant?
b) a butterfly?
c) a kitten?
d) a fish?
e) a monkey?

12. Would you cry if your pet died?

13. Which of the following is being cruel:
a) pulling the wings off a butterfly?
b) spraying a wasps' nest with insecticide?
c) overfeeding a pet cat?
d) keeping a social animal (such as a dog) away from others of its own species?
e) catching a fish with a hook and line?
f) keeping hens in a battery cage?

14. You find your best friend being cruel to a pet animal. What would you do?

15. Is it worse to:
a) steal a car or steal a pet animal?
b) mistreat a kitten or mistreat a baby?
c) call someone 'an animal' or 'a bastard'?
d) underfeed a dog or overfeed it?

16. If you could choose one animal to be sacred and protected for ever, which would you choose? Why?

17. You are given the power and money to 'solve' one animal issue (such as animal experiments, battery hens, circus animals, etc.). Which would you choose?

18. What's the worst thing you've ever done to an animal? What's the kindest? If you had your time again, would you still do them?

19. Under which of these circumstances do you think it's legitimate to kill the animal:
a) a tiger is about to pounce on you?
b) a mosquito is bothering you?
c) a herd of deer is severely damaging a forest by eating the trees?
d) a horse is too old to work?
e) a dog is homeless and stray?

   If you answered 'yes' to any of these, could you kill the animal yourself?

20. You are walking through a car park on a very hot day and you see a dog shut in a car with no air and in the hot sunlight. What would you do?

Humans and other animals

Three grey whales, trapped under the Arctic ice in Alaska, became the focus of a remarkable rescue mission in autumn 1988. They did what politicians could never do at the time – they brought together the Soviet and American armed forces. They were doomed to die there unless they could get to the surface for air, and their plight became a headline news story around the world. A joint Soviet-American rescue team was launched to save them, and thousands of dollars were spent cutting through the ice to give them air and make a channel to the open sea. The world breathed a sigh of relief as the three whales swam away to resume their migration south.

Over the same period, around the world, millions of animals died at the hands of humans – in experiments, traps and abattoirs, or when their habitat was destroyed. Most humans were indifferent to their suffering. What a strange species we are. We worship, pamper and admire some animals while others are reviled, tortured and destroyed.

Maybe one reason why humans abuse animals is that we cannot feel what it is to be an animal. We have forgotten that we are animals too. In Western societies, it's quite easy to lose touch with the natural world. Animals are becoming increasingly remote in our lives as more and more of us live in cities and machinery has taken over many of the jobs once done by animals. Our food is bought in a supermarket in tidy packages that give little indication of their animal origin – it's sometimes hard to realise that a hamburger was once a cow.

Humans – top dogs?

Most of us are brought up to believe that humans are the most important and most intelligent life on earth and are therefore superior to other animals. Some people translate this into a belief that people have power over animals and can use them as they wish. Others translate it into a responsibility to protect and care for other animals.

But is it true that we are superior to other animals, or are humans just being arrogant? In humans the brain and intelligence are highly developed, but other animals have different skills such as detecting magnetic fields or vibrations. Maybe we don't value these skills as much because they're not human ones.

Humans may appear very powerful as they dig tunnels under the English Channel, fire men into space and use modern technology to change the world in all sorts of ways. But however powerful we are, we cannot afford to forget that we cannot live without using other animals in some way. Without other animals humans could not exist at all. Animal and plant species on earth are part of a complex web of life. They provide food and energy for other plants and animals. They are essential parts of the natural cycles that give us fresh air, fresh water and a fresh supply of nutrients. Because we rely on other animals and plants for our own survival, it is in our interest to treat them with care and respect. Our dependence on animals goes further than this. We use them for profit, food, clothing, tools, entertainment, sport; to improve our image, our femininity or masculinity.

Animal rights or human responsibilities?

What sort of deal do we want to give other animals? The whole idea of animal rights is a controversy in itself. Is there any such thing as rights? Are rights a human concept and therefore irrelevant to animals? These debates rage on endlessly in philosophical circles, and while they're important in establishing the status of animals in a world controlled by humans, we also need to think about our responsibilities towards animals, and their needs.

Responsibilities to other animals fall into two categories: there are moral responsibilities such as 'should we experiment on animals to benefit humans?' and practical responsibilities such as 'how do we slaughter animals for food so that they feel as little pain and distress as possible?'

The important thing to remember about responsibilities is that they don't belong to other people – they belong to each one of us. It is a personal matter to face up to the issues and look at our own behaviour and beliefs. This book aims to help you do this by looking at some of the dilemmas surrounding humans and other animals.

The ten commandments

In his book *The Animal Contract*, the zoologist Dr Desmond Morris suggests ten commandments for humans to observe in relation to other animals. These ten commandments are:

1. No animal should be endowed with imaginary qualities of good or evil to satisfy our superstitious beliefs or religious prejudices.

2. No animal should be dominated or degraded to entertain us.

3. No animal should be kept in captivity unless it can be provided with an adequate physical and social environment.

4. No animal should be kept as a companion unless it can adapt easily to the lifestyle of its human owner.

5. No animal species should be driven to extinction by direct persecution or by further increases in the human population.

6. No animal should be made to suffer pain or distress to provide us with sport.

7. No animal should be subjected to physical or mental suffering for unnecessary experimental purposes.

8. No farm animal should be kept in a deprived environment to provide us with food or produce.

9. No animal should be exploited for its fur, its skin, its ivory, or for any other luxury product.

10. No working animal should be forced to carry out heavy duties that cause it stress or pain.

These ten commandments can help us look at our relationship with other animals and provide us with a code which would ensure that we respect them. It is neither sentimental nor stupid to recognise the relationship between ourselves and other animals, nor to feel that it is time they had a better deal. As far as we know, life exists only on the earth. We share it with other plants and animals – they are our fellow travellers.

Action guide

Each entry in the book has a 'What can you do?' section which gives specific ideas for action on that subject. Here are more general hints on what you can do. They can be applied to any subject, not just to animal rights and welfare.

Making your views known

To decision-makers:

Politicians do take notice of their mailbag because it reflects public opinion and they want the public to vote for them. You can write to or telephone:

- your Member of Parliament (MP), Member of the European Parliament (MEP), Ministers of State and even the Prime Minister;
- headquarters offices of political parties;
- your local councillors and council officials;
- ambassadors of other countries.

To the media:

The media are always looking for news stories, articles and letters to publish. You stand more chance of getting your message across locally, but it's worth trying the national media too. You can write to or telephone:

- local newspapers, free newspapers, parish magazines, school or college magazines;
- local radio;
- national newspapers and magazines;
- national television and radio programmes (write to the producer of the programme concerned) or the Duty Officer, BBC Television – or whichever station it is.

To companies and organisations:

These are the people who make the products we buy or provide us with services: if you're not happy with something, you can write to or telephone:

- the managing director or public-relations department of a company or organisation;
- school governors, parent–teacher associations, teachers and headteachers, or university or college heads of departments or the vice-chancellor.

Finding names and addresses:

To write or ring you need an address or telephone number, and it's useful to have a named person to contact if you can. You can find out this information from:

- public libraries – they have reference sections full of directories of newspapers, companies and organisations. They can also tell you who your MP or MEP is. It is the librarian's job to assist the public, so ask for help if you need it;
- your MP at the House of Commons and your MEP at the European Parliament (addresses in directory on page 135);
- telephone directories (other area directories are held in libraries);
- address lists in books, such as the one at the end of this book;
- newspapers and magazines, which have their address and phone number in them. With magazines it's usually at the

front; with newspapers it may be on the letters page or sometimes on the back page. You may have to search for it;

- *Radio Times* and *TV Times*, which list television and radio programmes; the names of the producers are also there. Addresses of television and radio stations can be found at the public library.

Inform and educate

First and foremost, inform and educate yourself so you know what you're talking about. You can do this by:

- reading books, magazines and leaflets;
- watching relevant television programmes and listening to radio programmes;
- talking to other people at meetings and discussion groups.

Warning: Don't believe everything you read or are told. Try to sort out whether information is fact or opinion, and take into account the interest of the person or group informing you.

A lot of people contribute to animal abuse and suffering through ignorance – they simply don't know what goes on, or the effect of their actions. You can help inform them by:

- putting up posters or distributing leaflets (many animal organisations produce these);
- speaking out in discussions and meetings – and organising them in your school, college, church, youth club or whatever;
- talking to friends.

Support voluntary organisations and charities

Organisations and charities working for animal welfare are always in need of support. You can do this by:

- joining them – many have reduced membership fees for young people; you also usually receive a magazine or newsletter which keeps you up to date on news and campaigns;

- giving them a donation;
- raising money for them through sponsored walks, jumble sales, house-to-house collections, etc. Many organisations can help you with this – contact them first.
- distributing leaflets or putting up posters;
- doing voluntary work for them, either locally or at their national office – again, contact them for details;
- buying goods from their catalogues for presents or for yourself – many have a good selection of publications, clothing, jewellery, badges, stationery and other goodies for sale.

Look at the way you live

Check out what you're doing in your everyday life. There may be many things you do out of habit which you could easily change and which would help animal welfare. The A–Z section of this book can give you lots of ideas here, but in general:

- think about what you eat, wear and buy;
- how do you treat your pets (if you have any) and other animals you come into contact with (this includes insects, birds, fish, etc.)?;
- challenge your own thinking – what have you been taught to believe? Is it true? Who says? Consider other points of view – look at the questions on page xi to give you a start;
- support the subjects which move you – those you *want* to take action on rather than those you feel you ought to support.

Facing up to criticism

Some people will admire you for taking action and living out what you believe is right, but there will be others who will criticise you. They may do this because they feel threatened, guilty, envious, or for a host of other reasons. But remember their feelings belong to them, not you – so try not to let them get to you. You are responsible only for what *you* do and feel.

Everybody is different, and we all decide what actions we want to take. You might wear leather shoes, yet be a vegetarian. If this is OK for you, that's fine. You draw the line where it's right for you. You don't have to be perfect or consistent, and you can make mistakes. But respect what other people do – it may not be the same as what you do, but they are different from you.

Don't get depressed

It can be depressing and overwhelming when you see what humans do to other animals and to other humans. Rather than sink into doom and gloom and feel helpless about the scale of abuse, you can do something. Look at the 'Action guide' or 'What can you do?' sections and choose something you feel you can do, however small it may be, which will contribute to change. You may not be able to see the change at the time, but every action helps. Feel good about what you do rather than bad about what you don't do.

How to use this book

The aim of this book is to bring together all the major animal rights and welfare issues facing our society today. About 86 topics are covered. Each topic has a short summary giving the basic information and raising some of the questions surrounding the issue. There are also practical suggestions for changing your lifestyle or putting your point of view across. The topics are arranged in alphabetical order, and you will find a complete list on page vii.

You don't have to read through the book in any particular order. You can dip into it, read it backwards or forwards, or look up individual topics that interest you.

WORDS IN SMALL CAPITAL LETTERS refer to another entry in the book where you can find further information. For example, under the BLOOD SPORTS entry you will find ANGLING, BIG GAME HUNTING, HUNTING and SHOOTING in small capital letters. This means there are also entries on those topics.

What can you do?: Each topic contains suggestions under a 'What can you do?' section. If you find that a subject upsets you or makes you angry and you want to do something, choose the action that suits you best. You don't have to do them all; you don't have to do any. There is also an 'Action guide' on page xix which gives general ideas and tips for getting going and keeping going.

Organisations: Lots of organisations are mentioned throughout the book, especially in the 'What can you do?' sections. The addresses of these organisations and others are printed in alphabetical order in the 'Directory of organisations' on pages 135–50.

If you want to know more: Look in the book list on pages 151–7 for a selection of titles on animal issues. You can also find out more from the organisations listed in the directory. If you feel like a break from reading, there is also a list of organisations supplying videos or slidesets you can watch.

Advertising

Look at the adverts you see on billboards, in magazines and on television. Animals feature frequently in them. You may see tigers and lions prowling around a high-performance car, cats enjoying a warm coal fire, puppies playing with toilet rolls or chimps having a tea party. Animals are used in adverts because they symbolise something to us – tigers and lions are strong and powerful, cats are sensuous and comfort-seeking, puppies are appealing and playful, chimps are comical and can 'ape' many human actions. The advertisers hope that what they symbolise to us may be transferred on to the product they're selling so that we think one type of car, for example, is more powerful or macho than another.

Most animals used in the advertising business are specially trained performers. They are well cared for, and often their owners are well paid for the performance. But should animals be made to act like humans (see ANTHROPOMORPHISM) or made to look silly to sell products? Should they be used at all in adverts? In America some advertising agencies think not and have banned the use of animals in their adverts.

■ *What can you do?*

If you see an advert which you think degrades animals, you can write and protest to the following organisations. You need to tell

1

them when and where you saw the advert, and details of your complaint.

1. The Advertising Standards Authority (ASA) deals with adverts in newspapers and magazines, posters, cinema and videocassette commercials, and on leaflets and brochures. Its general rule is that all advertisements should be legal, decent, honest and truthful.

2. The Independent Television Commission (ITC) deals with television commercials. It says in its Code of Advertising Standards and Practice that no animal should be caused 'pain or distress in the cause of making any commercial' and 'no advertisement may contain anything that might reasonably be thought to encourage or condone cruelty or irresponsible behaviour towards animals'.

3. The editor of any magazine or newspaper.

4. The managing director of the company manufacturing the product being advertised.

The RSPCA is the organisation concerned with the welfare of animals used in advertising and the FILM AND ENTERTAINMENT industry. If you think cruelty has been used in an advert, you can seek advice from them.

Alternatives to animal experimentation

To reduce the number of experiments using animals (see VIVISECTION), there has been a lot of research into alternative techniques for testing the safety of products. Organisations involved in researching alternative methods hope, in time, to replace animals in experiments completely. They consider that too many animals are routinely used in experiments, that animal experiments can be inaccurate and misleading, and that there are strong moral reasons against using them.

They call for the three Rs: reduction, refinement and replacement. **Reduction** means finding ways to reduce the number of experiments and animals used in them. **Refinement** involves improving laboratory experiments so that they involve as little pain and stress to the animal as possible. **Replacement** calls for finding alternative techniques to animal experiments such as computer simulation programs, cell and tissue culture, which mimic what happens on human skin and organs, the use of human volunteers and donated human organs. They also want to set up a database of experiment results available to all researchers so that the same experiment would not need to be performed twice.

Animal Aid have launched a Humane Research Donor Card which can be carried by anyone who wishes to support the reduction in use of animals in medical experiments. The idea behind the card is that in the event of the card-carrier's death their tissues would be donated to medical research. This would reduce the need for animals to be used in some types of experiment. The card scheme has been supported by leading human tissue researchers, but before it can really get going, a well-co-ordinated system of storing the donated organs needs to be set up.

■ *What can you do?*

Contact Animal Aid for further information on the Humane Research Donor Scheme and a donor card if you'd like to carry one. Animal Aid recommend that young people discuss the issues with their family first.

You can become a volunteer for 'human guinea pig' cosmetic tests. The RSPCA have a list of volunteers which you can join – contact them for further details.

FRAME (Fund for the Replacement of Animals in Medical Experiments), the Dr Hadwen Trust for Humane Research, the Lord Dowding Fund, and the Humane Research Trust are the organisations in Britain working on this topic. They can help you with further information and you can support their campaigns.

For alternatives to dissection in schools and colleges, see DISSECTION. See also COSMETICS AND TOILETRIES, MEDICAL EXPERIMENTS.

Angling

About four million people go fishing in Britain – it is one of the most popular sports. Although it involves catching wild animals with a line and hook, many people don't consider it a BLOOD SPORT – maybe because FISH cannot express pain in ways that humans, as mammals, understand. If fish screamed with pain, would angling be so popular?

Animal welfare organisations believe that fish do experience pain and stress, and that angling involves suffering to the fish. For this reason they oppose fishing. They also say that handling a fish out of water can harm its delicate scales, causing it to die later. Also, other species, such as herons and mink, may be killed by anglers and gamekeepers to protect fish stocks. There is also the problem of discarded and lost fishing tackle. This dangerous LITTER can trap and kill wildlife.

Individual fishermen and fisherwomen may, or may not, believe that fish can feel pain, but the angling community point out that they almost always return hooked fish to the water unless they are for eating. They also recommend that anglers handle fish only with wet hands to reduce injury. If fish are for eating, they say they should be swiftly and efficiently killed. The fishing community have also played a large role in fighting to prevent pollution in rivers, canals and other fishing waters.

■ What can you do?

Think about what your views are on fishing. You can get further information from the National Federation of Anglers or the Campaign for the Abolition of Angling. If you know any anglers, you could discuss the issues with them.

If you are opposed to angling you can support the Campaign for the Abolition of Angling. They publish information sheets and also have leaflets you can distribute.

Keep an eye on any local waterways, lakes or ponds for discarded fishing tackle. Clear it up carefully (there may be hooks!) and deposit it safely in a dustbin.

Animal Liberation Front

On Christmas Eve 1990, the Animal Liberation Front (ALF) broke into Oxford University's main cat-breeding unit, which provides cats for university experiments. The ALF took away 64 cats and took photographs of the conditions inside the breeding unit. In January 1991 they broke into Lancashire Polytechnic laboratories and took away 2 rabbits, 16 rats, 106 mice, one guinea pig and 43 doves as well as five sackfuls of documents.

These are examples of direct action on behalf of animals. They involve breaking the law, whether by breaking and entering private property or stealing the animals or documents inside. Sometimes these raids are carried out by the ALF, but there are also more extreme splinter groups operating such as the 'Animal Rights Militia'. They are well-organised undercover organisations working through small local groups or 'active units'. They can remain anonymous because they carry out their operations in total secrecy. These groups believe in:

- taking direct action to liberate animals from research laboratories, animal-breeding centres and sometimes from factory farms and provide them with decent homes;
- obtaining documents and publicising what is going on inside laboratories or farm units;
- damaging and destroying property used in animal exploitation.

Some of their members have been caught and are serving prison sentences for their part in a bombing campaign.

Many raids are non-violent but a series of bomb attacks on

laboratories, department stores selling fur and on the cars of research scientists has led many people to view the ALF and other animal liberation groups as terrorists. These violent acts have been condemned by most animal welfare and animal rights organisations who feel that violence in the name of animal rights is unthinkable and does their cause no good whatsoever. Animal Aid said in a statement after two car bombs exploded:

> We do not consider ourselves to be part of the same movement as those who entertain bombing other human beings . . . Those who terrorise or even sympathise with the terrorist can play no part in what we are striving to achieve.

■ *What can you do?*

Think about your views on non-violent and violent direct action. What do you think is the most effective way of bringing about change in the way our society uses animals?

There is another way of taking direct action – through PROTESTING legally and CHANGING THE WAY YOU LIVE. Read these sections for ideas on what you can do in your life to bring about change.

Animal rights

Some people believe that animals have rights; others do not. Opinions range from extreme views of total liberation for all animals to more practical ways of improving the relationship between animals and humans. It is up to each of us to look at the arguments and make our own decision about where we stand.

The case for animal rights

Non-human animals have many similar needs and feelings to human animals. They feel pleasure, pain, hunger and fear; they feed, mate and rear young, groom themselves and communicate with each other. The famous naturalist Charles Darwin said, 'There is no fundamental difference between humans and the higher mammals in their mental faculties.' Humans and other animals just have different skills. A human can write poetry, which other animals cannot do, but an Arctic tern can navigate from the Arctic to the Antarctic without map or compass, which a human cannot do.

Therefore, if we give rights to humans (which we do), we should also give them to other animals. Not to give animals rights is to discriminate against them because they are not human (see SPECIESISM).

We think it is wrong to treat humans as products or tools, or to use them as slaves – so it should be with other animals. Animal rights activists say all animals, including humans, have a moral right to be treated with respect and without exploitation. They call for justice, for an end to exploitation of animals in all areas where humans and animals interact, such as farming, sport and scientific research; and for compassion.

There is also an environmental argument for changing our attitudes to non-human animals. They are our fellow travellers on the earth, and we are all animals together on the planet linked through a common past. The way we treat other animals is only a reflection of the way we treat the planet, ourselves, and fellow humans(see ENVIRONMENT).

The case against animal rights

Humans are different from other animals. They are more intelligent; they can reason, make and use sophisticated machines and tools; they have highly developed languages and can communicate complex ideas to one another. They are superior to other animals.

How can you give rights to non-human animals when rights are a concept they cannot understand? A pig cannot vote or have freedom of speech. Where do you draw the line with animal rights? Would you give rights to slugs, amoebae or living viruses?

Animals do not respect human rights. A snake may kill a human without care or concern for its victim. Why, then, should we respect any rights for the snake? Other animals also kill each other in the daily struggle for food and survival. Why should we be any different?

Only humans have souls. They have a God-given right to use other animals for their own purposes (see BELIEFS).

Many humans on earth are being exploited and abused in many countries. Their suffering demands our attention more than animal rights. Humans are more important. We should protect our own species.

■ *What can you do?*

Think about animal rights. Do you think animals have rights? If so, what rights? Are human rights more important? Do humans have any duties or obligations towards other animals?

There are lots of books and leaflets you can read – see the list at the end of this book. Animal Aid and the RSPCA can also help with further information.

Animal welfare

Animal welfare is different from animal rights. Animal welfare is concerned about compassion and care towards other animals, whereas animal rights is concerned about justice towards them.

Animal welfare looks at how animals are treated and ways in which their lives could be improved. It accepts that animals are used by humans, and tries to improve their lot. Animal rights says animals should not be exploited at all, and fights for their freedom.

Animal welfarists concentrate on the relationship between animals and humans. They are concerned about exploitation of animals and cannot always accept the ways in which humans use them. Animal welfarists are concerned about animal suffering – the individual suffering of individual animals, not just the 'threat to the species'. They believe that humans have a responsibility to respect and care for other animals, irrespective of whether or not they have rights.

■ *What can you do?*

Read the ANIMAL RIGHTS section too. If you're interested in animal welfare, find out more and support the work of the RSPCA, Compassion in World Farming, Animal Aid or any of the many organisations listed in the directory at the end of this book.

Anthropomorphism

Anthropomorphism is the human habit of attributing human characteristics or feelings to animals. Here's an example from *The Tale of Little Pig Robinson* by Beatrix Potter:

> Little Pig Robinson was a charming little fellow; pinky white with small blue eyes and a double chin, and a turned up nose, with a real silver ring in it. Robinson could see that ring if he shut one eye and squinted sideways. He was always contented and happy. All day long he ran about the farm singing little songs to himself.

Here a pig is acting and thinking as if he were human, doing things that no pig would naturally do. Examples of anthropomorphism are all around us, especially in books or films for children. The success of Walt Disney films is built on cute, appealing animals doing human actions. But what happens to an animal when it is portrayed with human qualities or actions? Do we still see it as a living animal with a natural lifestyle, or as a semi-human? Snakes in stories are usually bad, and furry bunnies are good. Does it help us or animals to label some good and others bad?

The reverse of anthropomorphism is treating animals as if they had no feelings at all. This can cause us to see and behave towards them as if they were nothing but machines. Are battery hens egg-laying machines or living animals with feelings? Are we able to see animals as they are?

■ *What can you do?*

Be aware of examples of anthropomorphism on television, in films and in books. If you think it is unacceptable, you can write to the author via the book publisher or programme producer at the television channel, stating your point of view.

Aquaria

Aquaria displaying sea creatures provide a popular outing for people, particularly in seaside towns. Often people feel animals such as FISH, eels, whales and DOLPHINS are more at home in aquaria than zoo animals are in zoos. This may be because we are land mammals and know little about life in the sea. We find it easier to respond to other land mammals than to reptiles or fish.

The reality is that aquarium animals *are* in captivity in sterile environments. Sometimes their conditions are poor and their living space is very small. In the wild they live in social groups and range over huge areas. Sea mammals, particularly whales and dolphins, cover many thousands of miles in their lives and are highly social animals. Many sea creatures fail to breed in captivity – a sure sign of stress. Animal welfare groups have been campaigning to have sea mammals released from aquaria, safari parks and dolphinaria and have them rehabilitated (help them to adapt to life outside captivity) and returned to the wild. There are a few aquaria, however, where the owners have tried to create more natural conditions and where, for example, the humans are 'caged'. Visitors have to walk through glass tunnels in the middle of a large marine enclosure while the marine life swims around them.

Many aquaria have shows of performing sea mammals, usually dolphins, whales or porpoises. The social skills, intelligence and playfulness of these animals are used to full advantage. They learn quickly and willingly, and there is no need for cruelty in training them. In fact, the activity stops captive animals becoming bored. But are these animals no more than unpaid performers? Do we have a right to make them perform silly tricks for our amusement? Do they have a right to dignity and a natural existence? Aquaria, as well as zoos, raise the whole question of animals in captivity.

■ *What can you do?*

Consider whether you want to visit an aquarium, safari park or dophinarium. It is paying visitors who keep these places in business.

If you disagree with keeping sea creatures in aquaria, write to the local council where the aquarium is located, expressing your concern about keeping sea creatures in captivity and giving the reasons why. Ask them to refuse to license the aquarium in future. You can also write to the local newspapers.

Support the campaigns of Zoo Check, the Captive Animals Protection Society and the Whale and Dolphin Conservation Society. They can provide you with further information too.

See also TROPICAL FISH, WHALING.

Badger-baiting

Badger-baiting has been unlawful in Britain since 1911, but it still goes on illegally in many country areas. Badgers are dug out of their burrows (setts) and chained to a stake or put in a pit. They are then set on by dogs – often terriers – in a fight to the death. Sometimes the badger's jaws or teeth are broken by the baiters to improve the dogs' chances. Another 'sport' is badger-drawing, where the badger is put into a box or pipe and a series of fighting dogs are sent in after it to drag it out. The dog which does this the fastest wins.

As well as the 1911 law, there are plenty of other laws to protect badgers. The 1973 Badgers Act makes it an offence for anyone other than the landowner to dig badgers from setts or to kill or injure them, and the 1981 Wildlife and Countryside Act also includes badgers. In 1991 the Badgers Act was passed, making it an offence to damage, destroy, obstruct or cause a dog to enter a badger sett, or to disturb a badger in residence.

■ *What can you do?*

If you know of, or see, anything suspicious (such as men with terriers and spades in a woodland area) take the details of the car numbers and descriptions of the men and dogs, and call the police immediately. DO NOT APPROACH THE MEN, as they may be violent.

Contact your local county naturalists' trust (address from the

Royal Society for Nature Conservation) or local badger group (address from the National Federation of Badger Groups), who will know the badger situation in your area. They may want volunteers to help monitor setts.

Contact the League Against Cruel Sports for further information, and support their campaigns.

Beliefs

People have different opinions about animals. Some care passionately about animal welfare, while others are quite happy to hunt or kill them. How can two people, maybe living in the same house, come up with such fundamentally different views? Because they have different beliefs about animals. For example, a vegetarian may believe that animals have a right to their own lives, whereas a hunter believes they are on the earth to provide humans with food.

Beliefs are shaped by the attitudes of our family, our society, our schooling, our religion, and by countless other life experiences from birth onwards. Because we are all unique, each of us has our own unique set of beliefs. Differences in beliefs can be food for exciting and stimulating discussions, and for personal exploration. They can also be the source of conflict and war. Many people are convinced that their belief is the only correct one – the only truth. This can be dangerous if it is carried to extremes – for example, by eliminating all opposition. It is important to respect other people's point of view, even if you do not agree with it. Explain why you think they are wrong and listen to why *they* think *you* are wrong. You may both benefit!

Beliefs help to form our moral codes. Morals are concerned with human behaviour. Are actions good or bad, right or wrong? We have our own personal moral codes and standards of behaviour which are self-imposed, as well as those imposed on us by society. The majority of people abide by society's rules and accept that those who don't will be punished. The way society treats its animals reflects the beliefs and moral codes of the people in that society. Mahatma Gandhi, the Indian political and spiritual leader, said, 'The greatness of a nation and its moral progress can be measured by the way its animals are treated.'

■ *What can you do?*

We often don't know what our beliefs are until we think hard about them. Even then it's difficult, because they are complicated issues and we can often become confused with all the different points of view. As you read through this book, try to think about your beliefs and identify what some of them are. The questions in the introduction may help you as well.

Explore your beliefs by talking to others and finding out what they believe. Remember, you have to be guided by what you believe to be right.

Big game hunting

Big game hunting stirs up images of Victorian hunters shooting tigers in India. In the past, big game hunters have killed massive amounts of wildlife in Africa and Asia. Hunters were portrayed as brave and fearless men (and sometimes women) tramping through the bush and pitting their wits against ferocious beasts.

Although big game hunting has declined, it still goes on in some African countries where tourists can pay to go on hunting safaris. These safaris are promoted by government organisations keen to attract tourists and foreign currency into their country. The Tanzania Wildlife Corporation offers tourists more than fifty species of animal to hunt. The animals are hunted as part of a carefully controlled culling programme to reduce the size of herds. This is usually done by killing the weak, sick and old animals.

Big game tourism has provoked controversy over whether it is right to take pleasure in killing and continue big game hunting traditions. Should culls be done only by game reserve wardens? The safaris and tourists also continue the demand for wildlife souvenirs such as skins, heads, hoof key rings and stuffed animals.

Safari ranches in Canada and the USA are another development in game hunting. This 'sport' is more popularly known as 'canned hunting'. Game animals are specially bred or acquired from other – often illegal – sources, and hunters pay big money to kill them. Birds are the victims in many canned hunts, but if you're prepared to pay you can kill almost anything including zebra, black bear, oryx, lion and leopard. Business is booming, and there are about 4,000 hunt promoters supported by about half a million hunters. Some animals roam on huge ranches, but most are kept captive in cages or corrals. They are released into a pen, often no bigger than a football field, where they can be killed. Although this is promoted as hunting, many animals are killed less than 100 metres from their cage! The most popular weapons used are handguns, muskets, longbows and crossbows.

■ *What can you do?*

If you notice advertisements for hunting holidays, you can write to the travel companies involved and protest. Don't travel with these companies on any other holidays.

Don't buy curios and souvenirs made from wild animals, either in this country or abroad.

See HOLIDAYS.

Blood sports

Hunting once meant survival for humans. For some people in the world, it still does: if they don't hunt, they starve. With the domestication of animals and agriculture, it is no longer necessary in our society to hunt for food, but old instincts die hard. They now find an outlet in many sports, but especially in blood sports.

Blood sports (also called field or country sports) are those in which HUNTING is done for pleasure. They include SHOOTING, hunting with dogs, ANGLING, BIG GAME HUNTING and falconry. In Britain, there are also some illegal blood sports going on, including BADGER-BAITING and DOG-FIGHTING.

Hunting for sport takes a huge toll of wildlife around the world. It is difficult to know exactly how many animals are killed, but

1989 estimates in the USA say that licensed hunters killed 50 million mourning doves, 25 million rabbits, 22 million squirrels, 4 million white-tailed deer, 250,000 coyotes, 21,000 black bears and 1,000 wolves. In Britain, estimates put the death toll at 240,000 foxes, 80,000 deer, 350,000 hares, 10,000 badgers and 28 million birds.

Many people find hunting and killing for sport and pleasure disgusting, but hunters say that they have as much right to kill as any other animals – this is 'nature's way'. They also say that those who object to blood sports are town-dwellers with little understanding of country life, and that hunting is a form of PEST CONTROL.

■ *What can you do?*

You can find out more about blood sports from the League Against Cruel Sports and British Field Sports Society. See also ANGLING, BADGER-BAITING, HUNTING, SHOOTING and TRAPPING for further ideas for action.

Bullfights

Bullfights are found mainly in Spain but also in Mexico, Latin America, Portugal and southern France. In Spain it is big business, providing 160,000 jobs. Bulls are specially bred for the ring, and thousands are killed each year. Bullfight enthusiasts see them as part of Spain's national culture and tradition as well as a demonstration of beauty, artistry, human (usually male) courage and daring against a fierce beast. They say the bulls are well cared for before the fight, and their deaths are no worse than they would be in the wild.

But the dice are loaded against the bull. The bull is kept in darkness before being released into the ring, so that it is confused and dazzled by the light. Although it is against the rules, the bull's eyes are sometimes smeared with vaseline to blur its vision, and its horns are often filed down. Once in the ring, it is first taunted with capes and lances to weaken it before the matador enters to perform the kill. He uses a narrow sword which is thrust between the animal's shoulder blades and into the heart, but few bulls are killed in one blow. Fights usually last about twenty minutes.

The horses used by the matador's helpers are also victims of bullfighting. They are padded for protection, but often this is not enough and they are gored by the bull. Many have to be slaughtered – those which survive are used again in other fights.

The popularity of bullfights seems to be growing, especially among young Spaniards. There were 1,039 bullfights in 1990, the highest number since 1975. Paradoxically, there is also a growing movement to ban bullfights. One town, Tossa de Mar on the Costa Brava, has been officially proclaimed the first anti-bullfight town in Spain. Most Spaniards do not go to bullfights – they are a minority entertainment – but bullfighting is heavily supported by tourists from other countries.

■ *What can you do?*

Write and protest to:

- The Spanish Ambassador, 24 Belgrave Square, London SW1X 8QA
- Spanish National Tourist Board, 57 St James's Street, London SW1A 1LD
- French Government Tourist Office, 178 Piccadilly, London W1
- Portuguese National Tourist Office, New Bond Street House, 1 New Bond Street, London W1
- Mexican National Tourist Council, 7 Cork Street, London W1

Write to your MEP (Member of the European Parliament) calling for a European ban on bullfighting (your public library can help with the name and address).

If you can choose where you go on holiday, think about whether you want to go to Spain. If you do go, don't go to a bullfight or buy bullfight souvenirs. Many bullrings stay in business because of the number of tourists who go to see the fights. Pass this information on to friends and family who may be going on holiday to Spain.

Write and complain to travel companies who include visits to bullfights on their tours or advertise them in their brochures. If you're going to Spain, don't travel with these companies.

Support the anti-bullfight campaign run by the World Society for the Protection of Animals. The RSPCA also have a free leaflet on bullfighting.

Changing the way you live

'Example is not one way to influence people, it's the only way.' This was the view of Albert Einstein, the great scientist and thinker. Setting an example and living your BELIEFS may be more important in the long run than high-profile publicity stunts. Changing the way you live can help other people understand your cause and see that it is possible to change the way *they* live.

Changes to society are brought about by thousands of people making their own personal changes. Not so long ago, it was quite acceptable to wear FUR coats, and only a few people thought it was wrong. They told people how they felt and organised or supported anti-fur campaigns, and the message got around. Today, 81 per cent of women think it is wrong to kill animals for their fur, and most fur shops in Britain have gone out of business.

Changing your life isn't easy, but it isn't as difficult as you might think.

■ *What can you do?*

Find out what is right for you. As you read through this book, look at the 'What can you do?' sections and think about which actions you'd like to take and which you are able to take. Don't worry about what other people do – that's up to them. We all draw the line in a different place, so your friend may become a vegan while you may want to eat organic meat. It's your life, so make the changes *you* want.

Take a step-by-step approach. Don't try and take on too much. You can't change everything overnight, so set yourself realistic targets such as 'This week I'll eat vegetarian sandwiches' or 'I'll write one letter a week'. If you like planning things, making charts and ticking things off, you can set your weekly or monthly targets out on a sheet of paper and stick it on your noticeboard or wardrobe door.

Feel good about making small changes rather than bad about doing nothing. Don't criticise yourself for not doing enough. It's easy to be overwhelmed by the scale of a problem, but you *are* doing something positive.

You don't have to justify what you do to anyone. You may find that people are very ready to question what you are doing and may try to criticise your position. If you enjoy putting your point of view across and having a discussion, that's fine, but don't feel you have to justify what you do to others. If you don't feel confident about discussing these things, you can say, 'This is what feels right for me at the moment'.

You can change your mind. There's no rule which says you can't change your mind, although many people think there is. Explore and experiment with ways of changing your life. Take on board those you like, or are easy, or you want to do. Change them if you want to.

Chickens

Chicken and chips, chicken curry, Kentucky Fried Chicken . . . chicken is one of the most popular meals, and in Britain we now eat ten times more chicken than we did in the 1950s. It has become a cheap source of meat for many people, with farmers supplying £1.5 billion worth of chicken each year.

Almost all chickens for meat are reared in broiler houses – huge sheds where the heating, lighting and ventilation can be controlled to produce maximum weight gain. The day-old chicks are fattened up on high-protein food, so they grow quickly. At first the birds have space to move around, but towards the end of seven weeks, when they are slaughtered, the floor of the broiler house is packed with birds. To prevent the spread of disease, medicines are given via vaccination or through the feed.

Chickens are slaughtered at the processing plant, and it is a highly mechanised business. When they arrive they are hung upside down on a conveyor belt before being stunned and killed by an automatic knife which cuts their neck. Six hundred and seven million broiler chickens were slaughtered in Britain in 1990. An increase of 10 per cent is predicted by 1997.

Animal welfare groups and some farmers are concerned that the whole process is so mechanised that it treats chickens as objects, not as living beings; that the rearing process is cruel; and that the stunning procedure is not reliable enough and birds are knifed while they are still conscious.

Broiler units are the price we pay for cheap and plentiful meat.

■ What can you do?

Have a look at what you eat and what takeaways you buy – do you need so much meat? Why not try a vegetarian meal instead?

If you like eating chicken, are you prepared to pay more for it to ensure that it comes from free-range birds? It is possible to buy free-range oven-ready chicken in several of the big supermarket chains such as Tesco, Marks and Spencer and Sainsbury's. It is unlikely that any takeaway food shops will be serving free-range chicken, but you could write to them and ask them to. *The Kind Food Guide* by Audrey Eyton (Penguin, 1991) lists sources of free-range and organic meat.

Find out more from Compassion in World Farming and Chickens' Lib, and you can support their campaigns.

Write to your MP expressing your concern about the conditions in broiler units.

Christmas

Christmas may be heralded as a time of peace and goodwill towards all humans, but what about animals? For millions of turkeys in Britain it means the end of a short and unnatural life.

Like most other animals farmed for meat, turkeys are usually a product of FACTORY FARMING. The promotion of turkey meat means that 33.5 million are slaughtered in the UK each year, 11 million at Christmas. Like chickens, turkeys are reared in huge sheds. Their beaks are partially cut off to stop them pecking other birds – behaviour that comes with overcrowding. They are bred and fed way beyond their natural weight, diseases are controlled by drugs, and mating is by artificial insemination. It takes about sixteen weeks to rear a turkey from birth to death.

Christmas may also mean abandonment for many pet animals given as presents and unwanted after the Christmas season is over, another performance of silly tricks for circus animals, and for foxes the traditional Boxing Day hunt.

■ *What can you do?*

Consider having a vegetarian Christmas dinner. If you want to, you may need to check out with the cook that it is possible. This may mean discussing it with your family or whoever you spend Christmas with. There are lots of very good vegetarian cookbooks in libraries and bookshops which have mouth-watering recipes for a special occasion. Many vegetarians have a nut roast because it goes well with all the traditional Christmas vegetables. Here's one easy-to-prepare recipe.

Quick and easy nut roast (serves 4)

2 tablespoons cooking oil
2 onions, peeled and chopped
1 clove garlic, peeled and crushed
8 oz chopped nuts (such as cashews, hazelnuts, peanuts, almonds, walnuts, or a mixture of these)
4 oz wholewheat breadcrumbs

2 tomatoes, chopped
2 eggs, beaten
1 tablespoon tomato purée
1 tablespoon lemon juice
1 tablespoon soy sauce (optional)
1 teaspoon mixed herbs
salt and pepper

Grease a loaf tin or casserole dish. Heat oven to 190⁰C/375⁰F/
Gas mark 5. Heat oil in large saucepan and fry onions, tomatoes
and garlic until soft. Add all the other ingredients and mix well.
Spoon into prepared tin and bake for 45 mins to 1 hour until it
feels firm in centre. Take out of oven, leave to cool for 5 minutes,
then turn out on to warm plate and cut into slices.

Remember, most mincemeat (for mince pies) contains suet
made from animal fat. You can find vegetarian mincemeat in
health shops. Wholefood and health shops are also the best source
of other vegetarian Christmas food.

Also at Christmas . . .

Avoid going to CIRCUSES or HUNTING – see sections on these. Also
don't buy or encourage anyone to buy PETS as a Christmas
present unless you are sure they will be well cared for.

When you are buying presents for your family and friends, go
for cruelty-free products such as cosmetics and toiletries not
tested on animals. Many animal organisations such as Animal
Aid, Lynx, British Union for the Abolition of Vivisection,
RSPCA, Compassion in World Farming, the Vegetarian Society,
Zoo Check and the League Against Cruel Sports produce a wide
range of mail-order goods, which make excellent presents. Some
of them also sell gift tokens, and most supply Christmas cards
with a message. Catalogues are available on request.

Circuses

The greatest show on earth? Jugglers, acrobats, trapeze artists,
clowns and flying buckets of water can be great entertainment,

and many circuses are pure fun. But there are also circuses which aim to entertain by making animals perform silly tricks and portraying humans, such as the lion tamer, as brave and daring. For these circuses the title 'the saddest show on earth' might be more appropriate.

When they are not performing, circus animals spend most of their lives shackled or confined to cages, or being transported round the country by lorry. One study says that lions and tigers were confined for over 90 per cent of their time in cages only just big enough to turn round in. Most animals, including humans, normally live in social groups. In captivity, circus animals are deprived of the social, physical and emotional contact they need, and this deprivation causes them to develop abnormal behaviour such as pacing, swaying, head-banging and biting themselves. This is called stereotypic behaviour – many would say they have just gone mad.

Animal welfare organisations also say that training animals to perform tricks nearly always involves cruelty, fear and punishment. Circuses deny this. What happens to animals that do not learn tricks well or become too old to perform? In most cases they are destroyed.

Circus animals include lions, tigers, elephants, chimpanzees, bears and zebra. Some of these species are endangered. Although some circus animals are bred in captivity, others are captured from the wild, making circuses part of the TRADE IN WILD ANIMALS.

Animals may not understand the concept of dignity, but is it acceptable for humans to laugh at wild animals being made to ride a bicycle or jump through a hoop? Is this entertainment?

■ *What can you do?*

Circuses exist because people pay to go and see them. Don't go to circuses which have performing animals, and suggest to your family and friends that they shouldn't either.

Write to your local paper and protest.

Ask shopkeepers, politely, not to put up posters advertising circuses. Put up anti-circus posters – the RSPCA produce some with the message 'A circus is no fun for animals', or you can make your own.

Write to the circus's licensing authority (in Britain the local authority of the area where the circus is held – the address will be in the local telephone book). Ask them not to license circuses in the future.

If you know who owns the land where the circus is held, you could write a polite letter to them explaining why you think they shouldn't allow circuses with animals on their land again.

DO NOT approach circuses direct or protest on the circus site. There have been several violent incidents between circus employees and animal welfare protesters.

The Captive Animals Protection Society (CAPS) works to ban circuses. Contact them for further information and support their campaigns.

Clothes

Although you might not immediately think of clothing as involving the use of animals, the truth is that animals are used to make clothes and in testing the chemicals used in them.

FUR and LEATHER are directly linked to killing animals; wool is an animal product too, although sheep are not killed in producing it. However, wool-producing sheep have been bred using GENETIC ENGINEERING techniques to produce more wool than they would naturally. Lambs are also tail-docked, ear-punched with markers or numbers and castrated, and in Australia they have their tail and some skin cut away to prevent infestation by blowfly. One-fifth of Britain's wool is imported from Australia.

Nearly all fabrics, as well as wool and leather, are treated or dyed with chemicals tested on animals to make sure they do not irritate human skin.

Cotton might seem the obvious alternative, as it is produced from a plant, but cotton crops are sprayed heavily with pesticides. Pesticides are also tested on animals, and they may not do the environment a lot of good either – they contribute to water, land and air pollution.

■ *What can you do?*

Do you want to wear animal products? Wearing clothes that involve killing animals, such as fur and leather, may be unacceptable to you, but wool may be OK. You may want to wear no animal products. Think about where you draw the line and decide what is right for you now. You can always change your mind as your ideas develop.

We all have to wear something, but clothing is an area where it's difficult to find alternatives to commercially produced fabrics and clothes. However, you can reduce the amount of new clothes you buy. Mend and repair your clothes rather than throw them out. Have a look in charity shops, where the clothes are usually in good condition, and much cheaper. You can have the satisfaction of both helping a charity and saving yourself money. You can also change your wardrobe more often. When you get bored with clothes, take them back and buy some more.

It's still nice to buy new clothes, and there is now a range of attractive and environmentally friendly cotton clothing which is not bleached, so reducing pollution and testing on animals. Greenpeace and Friends of the Earth sell them – sales catalogues are available. Animal Aid produce cruelty-free T-shirts and sweat shirts – the printing inks are not tested on animals, and they are made from unbleached cotton. The design and message also show the world that you support living without cruelty, and Animal Aid.

Controversy

A controversy is a debate or argument in which there is strong disagreement, usually carried out in public or in the press. Animal rights issues nearly always fit this definition. There is certainly strong disagreement between animal rights campaigners and research scientists, farmers, drugs or cosmetics companies. The debate is frequently carried out in the public eye through the media – newspapers, magazines, radio and television – and through demonstrations and campaigns.

Unfortunately, the debate is often portrayed as two sides opposing one another. Animal rights campaigners are presented as left-wing terrorists who will happily kill a child to save a rabbit; scientists or surgeons are presented as cruel monsters performing hideous experiments in secret laboratories. In between these two extremes are most animal campaigners – people who feel genuine sympathy and KINSHIP with animals. They don't want to break the system, they want a better deal for animals through non-violent and legal means. They make their point of view known by PROTESTING and by CHANGING THE WAY THEY LIVE.

Similarly, there are many scientists who are genuinely concerned about animal welfare. They would rather not use animals in research but believe they are doing their best for people.

It's easy to label people or stereotype them but, as usual, it's more complicated than goodies and baddies.

■ *What can you do?*

Be aware when you read newspaper reports or information from campaigning groups about these stereotypes. Keep an open mind!

See also EMOTIONS.

Cosmetics and toiletries

Cosmetics have a glamorous image. Adverts show beautiful models with flowing hair and no spots living exciting and romantic lives. This is what cosmetics manufacturers want us to associate their product with. What they don't want us to know is that most of their products have been tested on animals.

Companies are required by law to meet minimum health and safety standards for all chemical products or ingredients, which are screened for any harmful effects they might have when used by people. This is usually done by testing them on animals, although the law does not specifically call for animal tests. (The main tests used by cosmetics companies are explained under VIVISECTION.)

In 1989 over 12,000 animals were used in cosmetics testing in Britain. The number of tests is now slowly falling as manufacturers have come under pressure from animal welfare groups and concerned customers have turned to cruelty-free products. Many people now feel that animal testing is cruel and unnecessary, particularly for products such as shampoo, lipstick and hairspray, which are purely decorative. The success of The Body Shop and the introduction of cruelty-free brands into the big supermarket chains are just some indicators of this change in people's attitudes.

Some manufacturers have found alternative methods of testing, such as *in vitro* techniques (the use of tissue and cell cultures which mimic what happens on human skin and organs). Other companies, such as The Body Shop or Beauty Without Cruelty, have cruelty-free policies and use only well-tried and tested ingredients. If their products do require testing, human volunteers are used. However, many of the big and famous names in cosmetics still test on animals.

■ *What can you do?*

When buying cosmetics or toiletries, look on the label for the words 'not tested on animals' or 'cruelty-free', or the white rabbit logo. The Body Shop and Beauty Without Cruelty are two well-known cosmetics manufacturers who do not test on animals; most of their products are also VEGETARIAN and use only natural vegetable ingredients and harmlessly obtained animal products such as beeswax and honey. Many supermarkets have also stopped testing on animals – again, check the labels before you buy (see LABELLING).

If you can't find cruelty-free products in your local shop or supermarket, approach or write to the store manager, asking him or her to stock some.

If you like to buy favourite products which don't have cruelty-free labels, you can write to the public-relations department of the companies asking them how their ingredients are tested. Are they tested on animals in the UK or any other country by the company, its suppliers or a third party? If you receive an unsatisfactory answer, pursue them with another letter. If they admit to testing on animals, you can write again asking them to stop and boycotting their products (tell them you're doing this).

Support the campaigns of Animal Aid, The Body Shop, British Union for the Abolition of Vivisection, the National Anti-Vivisection Society and the RSPCA. All these organisations have information leaflets available.

BUAV and the RSPCA also produce an Approved Product Guide listing cosmetics and toiletries which are not tested on animals. *The Cruelty-Free Shopper* by Lis Howlett (Bloomsbury, 1989) is a handy paperback which lists products which do not exploit animals.

If you want more information on the cosmetics industry, contact the Cosmetics, Toiletry and Perfumery Association.

Take your own cruelty-free shampoo and conditioner to the hairdresser's, and tell them why. Many people just don't know about animal testing, so tell them and encourage them to buy cruelty-free.

Different cultures, different opinions

In India cows are sacred, so they are not slaughtered and eaten; many people are vegetarian. In Britain we are quite happy about killing and eating cows, but consider it offensive to eat dogs. In Korea, it is quite acceptable for people to eat dogs. Attitudes to animals differ around the world, according to the local customs and culture, and these are often based on religious BELIEFS.

This book is mainly about Western attitudes to animals, and these are based on Jewish-Christian culture. The Bible is the holy book, and in Genesis Chapter 1 verse 26 it says:

> Then God said . . . 'let them [humans] have dominion over the fish of the sea and over the birds of the air, and over the cattle, and over all the earth, and over every creeping thing that creeps upon the earth.'

For many centuries Christians interpreted this as a God-given right to do what they wanted with other life on the planet. As Christianity spread and cultures were shaped by it, this human superiority over the rest of nature became a widely held belief. Many people viewed nature as a force which had to be dominated and subdued. Today many people feel that these attitudes have been a root cause of many world environmental problems.

Many Christians over the centuries have not taken this view of nature and animals. St Francis of Assisi called other creatures his sisters and brothers, and recently there have been great changes in Christian thinking. 'Dominion' over animals has come to be interpreted as guardianship of rather than power over nature.

Other religions have very different views on animals and nature. In India, Hinduism is the major religion. Hindus believe that all forms of life have a soul and a right to exist. One of their holy books says:

> One should treat animals such as deer, camels, asses, monkeys, mice, snakes, birds and flies exactly like one's own son. (*Srimad Bhagavatam*, Canto 7, 14:9)

Buddhism also teaches non-violence, compassion and animals' right to live, and Jainism, another Indian religion, believes in non-violence to all living things. Jains are strict vegetarians and cannot be farmers because ploughing the soil might injure animals and plants.

Although cultures may tend to follow one or other set of beliefs, there are always individuals who don't, so you may find Hindus who eat meat, Christians who abuse animals and Christians who care for animals. There are also many people who do not believe in a God but show great care and concern for other living creatures.

■ *What can you do?*

Find out more. The World Wide Fund for Nature (WWF) has set up the International Network on Conservation and Religion, which brings together eight of the world's major faiths to discuss conservation and attitudes to nature. The Network publishes a free bulletin called *The New Road*, which is available from WWF International.

You can also find out more from the Christian Consultative Council on Animal Welfare, the Catholic Study Circle for Animal Welfare, the International Jewish Vegetarian Society, the International Muslim Association for Animals and Nature, and Quaker Concern for Animals.

If you are a churchgoer, many churches hold services for

animals on or near 4 October, World Day for Animals. You can speak to your vicar or priest and maybe contribute to the service. You could also put information about animal issues on church noticeboards, or ask for them to be discussed in home study groups.

Dissection in schools and colleges

Dissection was once commonplace in school biology and zoology lessons, and thousands of animals were killed to supply the specimens. Over recent years, dissection has played a diminishing role in schools. In the UK, exam boards do not require whole-animal dissection below A level, but it is still included in some A level syllabuses (although it is not usually compulsory). With some exam boards the decision to dissect is left to the discretion of the teacher; others set alternative papers for those who refuse to dissect animals.

Dissection, it is argued, is necessary to teach students a better understanding of lifeforms. It enables them to understand the internal structures of animals and to gain personal experience of these structures. In the past, many students have felt unhappy about performing dissections, but they have been a compulsory part of examinations. Students who did not want to take part were labelled 'squeamish' or 'soft' by some teachers.

Opponents of dissection in schools argue that dissection is a 'relic of the past' and that we can understand life better by studying it alive rather than dead. They also say that dissection undermines respect for life by treating other species as disposable educational tools.

Many alternatives to dissection have been developed, including computer simulations, books, charts, videos and models. There are several catalogues available listing them – see the book list at the end of this book.

However, many people still consider that dissection is essential to a career in medicine or veterinary medicine. Most higher-education courses in these subjects require students to perform dissections. The National Union of Students has launched a campaign to defend the right of any undergraduate to refuse, without fear of penalty, to carry out practical work on animals.

■ *What can you do?*

Early in the term, find out if you will be expected to dissect animals. If the answer is 'yes', this will give you time to think whether you want to do it. If you don't want to, it will give you time to read up and be fully prepared for any discussions on the subject. Animal Aid, the British Union for the Abolition of Vivisection (BUAV), the National Anti-Vivisection Society (NAVS) and the RSPCA produce information on dissection and exam board requirements. Animal Aid and BUAV also publish a step-by-step guide to refusing to dissect and petition forms so that you can enlist the support of your friends, parents and even teachers.

It's not easy to refuse to do what you are told to do by teachers or lecturers, but don't be intimidated. You have a right to refuse to perform dissections. If you are under eighteen, it's a good idea to have your parents' or guardian's support if you wish to object. This is because, legally, you have to be educated in accordance with your parents' wishes. You can put your point of view to your teacher, headteacher, school governors and local council. Liberty (the National Council for Civil Liberties) have pledged support for students' basic right to refuse without penalty.

You can inform your teacher and school about the alternatives available and the catalogues and handbooks listing them – see the book list.

You can inform your friends and fellow pupils about the situation.

You can join the Campaign for Violence-Free Science run by NAVS.

Dog-fighting

Dog-fighting is illegal in Britain, but it still goes on in secret locations.

Two dogs are put into a ring or pit together to fight each other.

There are usually fight rules and a referee. Injury to both dogs is usually severe, and the death of the loser often occurs. Survivors may need surgery and painkillers.

Terriers are the favourite fighting dog – especially English and Staffordshire bull terriers and the notorious American pit bull terrier. They are specially trained to develop a taste for flesh and blood, and to build up fighting stamina. Training may also involve fighting against wild animals such as badgers (see BADGER-BAITING).

Many dogs belonging to the fighting breed are kept as pets as well as guard dogs. Recently, unprovoked attacks on children by American pit bull terriers and other dogs led to a public outcry and a change in the law. The 1991 Dangerous Dog Act applies to pit bull terriers, Japanese tosas and several other breeds of fighting dog. These breeds must now be muzzled and on a lead in public places, registered, neutered and marked with owner's identification, or humanely destroyed. In Hamburg, Germany, breeds of dogs used for fighting now have to be licensed in the same way as guns.

■ *What can you do?*

The RSPCA Special Investigations Department are continually working, often in undercover operations, to locate dog-fights and prosecute the people involved. They encourage the public to give them any information which may help them track down fight venues or organisers. If, for example, you see people with terriers gathering at a barn or garage, or dogs with severe injuries, this may be a sign of fighting. Contact the police or RSPCA immediately. DO NOT APPROACH THE PEOPLE, as they may be violent.

Dogs

Man's best friend? There are 7.3 million dogs in Britain – some live lives of luxury as PETS; others work as guide dogs, police dogs or sheep dogs. But for a nation known as animal lovers, there are some sorry statistics. One thousand stray dogs are destroyed by the RSPCA each day, and convictions for cruelty to dogs have risen by over 60 per cent since 1989.

There are lots of animal welfare issues surrounding dogs.

Greyhounds: Winning racing dogs are prized animals, but there are many greyhounds who are not winners or become too old for racing. Recent investigations have revealed that some are being supplied to research laboratories in Britain and abroad for use in experiments (see VIVISECTION). There has been an outcry over this trade in dogs, and the National Greyhound Racing Club say that owners will be banned for life if they are found selling dogs to laboratories.

Puppy farms: These are large-scale dog-breeding farms to supply the pet trade in Britain and abroad. It is a thriving business. Some 'farms' are often no more than a collection of sheds and garages, and the conditions the dogs are kept in vary from good to appalling with tiny, dirty cages and inadequate food and exercise. Bitches may often be worn-out and stressed from continually producing litters. The puppies are often weak and easily develop illnesses.

The puppies are sold through networks of dealers – some are crated and exported abroad, but most go to pet shops or are sold through newspaper adverts.

Dog registration: The RSPCA have been campaigning for years for a national compulsory dog registration scheme which links each dog to its owner. Each owner would pay to be registered and have their dog electronically tagged. The RSPCA say this would make tracing stray dogs easier, reduce fouling of public places, make fighting-dogs and puppy farms easier to trace, and improve welfare for all dogs. In a public opinion poll 92 per cent of people asked supported the RSPCA scheme, but governments have so far refused to introduce it.

■ *What can you do?*

If you see or know of cruelty to a dog, report it to your local RSPCA inspector (see under 'Royal Society' in the telephone book).

Support the RSPCA campaign for a national dog registration scheme – you can find out more from them. Contact your MP and ask him or her to support the scheme too.

If you have a dog, make sure it has a collar and tag with your name, address and telephone number on, or have it electronically tagged (contact your vet or the RSPCA for further information).

If you want to get a puppy, don't go to a pet shop. If you buy through a newspaper advert, make sure you see the mother dog too so that you know the puppies are not from a puppy farm. Dog rescue homes have lots of puppies needing good homes. They also need support through donations, and often voluntary help. Contact your local dogs' home for more information.

Be a responsible dog owner. Dogs fouling footpaths and public places give both dogs and owners a bad name. Clean up after your dog with a 'pooper-scooper' (available from pet shops).

Dolphins

The relationship between dolphins and humans goes far back into history. In Ancient Greece dolphins were worshipped, and killing a dolphin carried the death penalty. Dolphins feature in many legends and stories. They symbolise freedom, friendship and playfulness.

There have been many recorded instances of dolphins helping humans by guiding boats and saving drowning people. These beautiful, intelligent, sociable wild mammals are now under extreme pressure from POLLUTION, hunting and, most seriously, from the fishing industry.

Millions of dolphins and other sea creatures die after becoming entangled in the many miles of fine-meshed nets – called drift nets – put out by commercial fishing vessels. The net is often called the 'wall of death'. Dolphins also die at the hands of tuna-fishing fleets. Yellowfin tuna congregate underneath groups of dolphins, and the fishing fleets use the dolphins to locate the tuna. They encircle the tuna and dolphins with nets, and in netting the fish they kill the dolphins too. About 7 million dolphins have been killed this way in the past thirty years. Scientists recently warned that dolphins and porpoises face extinction in some parts of the world because of the fishing industry's activities.

Dolphins have also been exploited by humans because of their intelligence and playfulness. They are kept in captivity in zoos and AQUARIA, where they often perform tricks in dolphin 'shows'. There is a high death rate for zoo dolphins, and debate rages on the morality of keeping such social, free-ranging and intelligent animals captive. Many animal welfare groups in Europe and the USA have been campaigning for the release of zoo dolphins, and some animals have been returned to the seas.

In a more sinister development, dolphins have been used by the US Navy for military duties such as guarding submarine bases and, it is rumoured, planting mines and even detecting enemy frogmen. This raises the question of whether humans are justified in using another animal for military purposes (see WARFARE). There have also been allegations of cruel training methods for these dolphins.

■ *What can you do?*

If you or your family eat tuna, make sure it is 'dolphin-friendly'. Many supermarkets and importers now ask for strict environmental standards from the tuna companies which supply them. Look for the words 'caught with pole and line' or 'caught with hook and line' on the label. This means the tuna hasn't been caught in nets.

Support the work of the Whale and Dolphin Conservation Society, the Marine Conservation Society, the Environmental Investigation Agency, Zoo Check or the Dolphin Circle. You can find out more information from them.

If you want to see a wild dolphin, dolphin-watching and dolphin-swimming holidays are available. They are usually advertised in wildlife magazines. If you are interested, read the HOLIDAYS section on eco-tourism first.

FREE RANGE

Eggs

Eggs feature in most of our diets, whether we eat them fresh or in quiches, cakes and puddings.

There are 38 million egg-laying birds in Britain, and 90 per cent of them are kept in the infamous battery units – large sheds with hundreds of wire cages stacked in rows six high. Each cage holds between 4 and 6 birds, and the average cage size is 18″ × 20″ (46 cm × 51 cm). Feeding, drinking and egg-collecting are automated. Battery units are a very efficient way of producing cheap eggs, but the cost to the birds is high.

A hen's natural instincts are to flap, perch, nest, dust bath and scratch the ground, but in the battery cage she can do none of these things. In fact she doesn't even have the space to stretch her wings. This chronic overcrowding causes extreme stress, resulting in aggression, cannibalism and pecking. To stop the birds pecking each other, they are de-beaked. After about a year of laying, they are killed to be made into chicken soup, paste or pet food. Only female chickens lay eggs, so each year 50 million male day-old chicks are gassed and ground up to make animal food.

The good news on battery cages is that their future is uncertain. They are being phased out in Switzerland and in some German states. A directive was passed by the European Commission to increase the cage size, and European welfare groups are running a vigorous campaign to ban the battery.

■ *What can you do?*

It is consumer demand that will make the industry change. If you do the shopping, don't buy battery eggs. It's difficult to tell which eggs are battery produced because they're not labelled and they may often have misleading names such as 'farm fresh' or 'country fields'. However, eggs from free-range hens are labelled 'free-range'. They are usually more expensive, but you know the hens have had a reasonably natural life. If you don't see them on the shelf, ask the shop manager if he or she will stock them.

Tell friends and family about battery units and suggest that they buy free-range eggs if possible.

You can write to your school or college catering department asking them to switch from battery to free-range eggs. Compassion in World Farming's (CIWF) youth section, Farm Watch, are campaigning for this, and can give you further help.

Support the campaigns by CIWF and Chickens' Lib – car stickers, posters and information sheets are available. You can also find out more from the Free-Range Egg Association (FREGG).

You can write to your MP and/or the Minister of Agriculture, calling for a ban on battery cages.

See also FOOD FEARS.

Emotions

Emotions are a powerful force, and animal issues often provoke strong emotions in people – compassion or cruelty, anger or sadness, pleasure or torment. It follows, then, that animal rights issues also provoke strong feelings.

Opponents of animal rights accuse the animal campaigners of manipulating people's emotions by using shock-horror photos and stories, or by appealing to their attraction to cuddly and furry animals. They say campaigners go for the heart and emotions and don't use reason in their arguments. In reply to this, animal campaigners quote the philosopher Jeremy Bentham, who said (in 1789!), 'The question is not, Can they *reason?* nor Can they *talk?* but, Can they *suffer?*'

In return, animal campaigners accuse scientists of being cold and emotionless; of appealing only to the head and intellect.

Emotions are important because they are the stuff of life. They also motivate people to take action. But when dealing with controversial and difficult questions such as animal issues, balance is needed. Clear thinking, together with a feeling heart, make a winning combination.

■ *What can you do?*

Most of us are trained from childhood not to express emotions such as anger, fear, compassion, sadness and sexual feelings, so it's often difficult to know or show what you are really feeling. When you read through other sections of this book, try to be aware of the emotions you feel.

Endangered species

There are estimated to be between 5 and 8 million different animal and plant species on earth. Humans are one of them. It is quite natural for species to die out (or become extinct); this is part of evolution. However, as humans have become the dominant species on the planet, the rate of extinctions has become faster than the rate at which new species evolve. About one species is lost each day, mainly through destruction of their habitat, HUNTING or POLLUTION.

Habitats are lost as land is taken for agriculture, mining, forestry and building. The human population has soared, and in some areas there is simply not enough land for humans and wildlife to live together. Pollution also kills animals. The Mediterranean monk seal has been reduced to 190 individuals because of pollution and loss of habitat.

The ruthless hunting of species has caused the near-extinction of many animals such as the black rhino. Animals are often hunted to provide luxury goods such as ivory carvings, crocodile-skin handbags or FUR coats.

Over eighty countries, including the UK, have signed the Convention on International Trade in Endangered Species (CITES) to help conserve wildlife threatened by international TRADE IN WILD ANIMALS. CITES classifies over 500 species in which trade is banned. There are also further regulations, set by the European Community, on importing and exporting endangered species.

We tend to think of endangered species as furry mammals such as pandas or tigers, but insects, reptiles, fish, birds and plants are also under threat. It is also tempting to conserve only those species which might be useful to humans as food, fur or medicine. Is the only justification for conserving an animal the fact that it is useful to humans? Don't animals have a right to exist just for what they are – not for their usefulness?

■ *What can you do?*

You may not realise which goods come from endangered species, so the safest rule is to avoid buying anything made from wild animals and birds. This includes: furs and skins such as reptile-skin bags, shoes, belts and wallets; carved ivory; shells; tusks or horn handles on knives; feather or butterfly products. Think about what you buy.

Watch out when buying tourist souvenirs abroad. If you bring any items made from endangered species into Britain, you could have them confiscated at Customs. The Department of the Environment (DoE) Endangered Species Branch produces a free leaflet which explains the law.

If you see shops selling wild-animal products in your area, you could write to them explaining the situation and asking them to stop. If you get no response, you can get advice and more information from the DoE Endangered Species Branch.

Environment

Environmental issues have made a huge impact on the press and the public in the last few years after a series of environmental disasters such as the *Exxon Valdez* oil spill, the Chernobyl nuclear power station explosion and the destruction of the tropical rainforests. We depend on the environment for everything. If we damage it, we damage ourselves. The environment is more than wildlife and wild places; it is not just 'out there'. It is everything, including humans *and* other animals and plants, wilderness *and* cities, oceans, air *and* land. Caring for the environment means caring for other animals, for other humans, and for ourselves. We are all on this earth together – we are all connected. Without a healthy environment, humans will not be healthy either.

Many people in Western societies have lost the feeling of being connected to other lifeforms on the planet. Many TRIBAL PEOPLES have never considered it a possibility that they're not. They feel a spiritual connection between themselves and the environment. This is part of a very famous statement by Chief Seattle, a Native American Indian:

> All things are connected. This we know. The earth does not belong to man. Man belongs to the earth . . .

Attitudes to the environment are changing, and people and governments all over the world are beginning to respond to what Margaret Thatcher, Britain's former Prime Minister, called 'one of the great challenges of the late twentieth century'.

■ *What can you do?*

Thoughts and feelings connected to the earth must be backed up by practical action: CHANGING THE WAY YOU LIVE and using less of the world's valuable resources. There are many things you can do in your everyday life. For starters you can reduce the amount of waste you create, use less energy or recycle paper, glass and tins. There are many excellent books on how to be green, such as *The Young Person's Guide to Saving the Planet* by Debbie Silver and

Bernadette Vallely (Virago, 1990) – see also the list at the end of this book.

Find out more from the many environmental organisations such as Friends of the Earth or World Wide Fund for Nature. See also JOINING GROUPS.

Factory farming

Imagine a farm. You may have an image of a country farm with chickens scratching in the yard and animals grazing peacefully in the fields. This is also an image you are likely to see in books, in adverts and on television. There are some farms where animals can 'free-range', but on many more the picture is very different. Most farm animals spend all their lives indoors in 'farm units', where they are tethered or caged. They will leave only to be slaughtered. Because of the similarity to a production line in a factory, this type of farming has been christened 'factory farming'. It is also sometimes called 'intensive farming'.

Intensive systems mass-produce animals. They use less land, less labour, and the turnaround of animals from birth to death is faster than in free-range farming. Factory farms are used widely in Europe, North America and Australia, where labour and land are expensive. Some farmers are concerned about factory farming, but others maintain that it is not cruel and that animals are healthy and well cared for. They say factory farming produces plenty of meat at an affordable price.

Animal welfare groups object to factory farming because it treats animals as meat or egg machines. Animals do not have the opportunity to behave naturally – running, rolling, touching, stretching. This causes stress and disease, conditions which are then treated with a variety of drugs and chemicals which may remain in meat. They say that farm animals are feeling, intelligent, living beings and deserve to be treated as such.

This is our responsibility to the animals that are killed for our food.

■ *What can you do?*

If you eat meat, whether it's in a hamburger, a Sunday roast or a curry, you are most probably a consumer of factory-farmed products. Think about what you eat, and if you want to change. Maybe you are not in control of what is cooked in the household, and feel you cannot change at the moment, but if and when you have a choice you could reduce your intake of meat by becoming a VEGETARIAN, even if it's for only one day a week.

If you like meat too much to give it up, try to persuade your family to buy organic or 'free-range' meat (see FOOD WITHOUT CRUELTY).

You can find out more from Compassion in World Farming and the RSPCA. They run many campaigns demanding better conditions for farm animals which you can support by letter-writing. The Farm Animal Welfare Council and the Athene Trust also have information about farm animal welfare.

Write to your MP, your MEP (Member of the European Parliament) and the Minister of Agriculture, asking them for their views on factory farming and calling on them to ensure that every farm animal has the freedom to move around, groom itself, stretch its limbs and exercise freely.

Because factory farms are out of sight, they are also out of most people's minds. Tell your family and friends what you think, and make them aware of the real price of cheap meat.

See also CHICKENS, EGGS, PIGS, VEAL.

Films and entertainment

Animals are featured in films, television programmes and commercials (see ADVERTISING). Sometimes, like Lassie, they become the stars; at other times they are part of the supporting 'cast'. Now there are strict regulations about the use of animals in the entertainment industry, but it used to be a different story.

In many old films animals were treated cruelly or even killed for the sake of the plot. In America, one film changed this. In 1937 the film *Jesse James* showed two horses being ridden over a cliff into the sea, but the horses used to perform this stunt had to be destroyed afterwards because they were so badly injured. This act of cruelty caused an outcry and led to the setting up of guidelines to protect animals used in the film industry by the American Humane Association (AHA). Today the AHA is very active in the American entertainment industry. When any animals are to be used, they check the script and have a representative on the set during filming. Their guidelines cover all animals, including fish and insects. In the UK, the RSPCA undertake the same task as the AHA. They also advise the Board of Film Censors so that scenes of cruelty do not reach the cinema screen.

Dances With Wolves, the 1991 Oscar-winning film, set new standards on animal welfare in films. The film has several scenes of buffalo hunts, and to ensure that no animals were killed or injured during filming, twenty-three fake buffalo were created. Others were trained to stampede. Good training is the essence of using animals in films, and many trainers work to the highest welfare standards.

■ *What can you do?*

The film industry is so expert at creating special effects that it's difficult to know what is a real act of cruelty. If you are unhappy about a scene, you can seek advice from the RSPCA. If you know the film involves cruelty you can not only refuse to see it but also write to the cinema manager explaining why.

Write to local and national newspapers and film magazines pointing out scenes of animal abuse and calling for people to boycott these films.

The Broadcasting Standards Council monitor 'the portrayal of violence, sex and matters of taste and decency' in television and radio programmes. Violence to animals is covered in their code of practice. If you see a scene which you think degrades or is violent to animals, complain to them as soon as possible. State where and when you saw or heard the programme, and the details of your complaint.

Fish

It is difficult for many humans to feel any connection with fish. They are not like us; they are cold-blooded creatures that live in water. We are warm-blooded and live on land. They do not show emotions that we understand; they do not scream in pain or show signs of stress we recognize. Because of this, many humans show less care and compassion for fish, but fish are very sensitive animals. They are sensitive to fear, stress, taste, smell, noise, light and dark. They communicate, often live in social groups, and have young.

All around the world, fish are killed in their millions. About 80 million tonnes are caught every year, and they are a major food source for many of the world's people. However, one-third of the world's fish catch is fed to animals or used as fertiliser on the land. The fishing industry has overfished the oceans severely, reducing the populations of some species such as herring and pilchard. All manner of methods are used to get fish out of the water, including 'hoovering' them up wholesale with factory ships, blowing them out of the water with explosives, catching them with hook and line or in nets.

There has been a lot of publicity about DOLPHINS being caught in fishing nets, but what about the fish themselves? Netted fish die by suffocation, crushing, thermal shock when they are dumped into freezing tanks of brine (salt water), or from ruptured swimbladders. These are not quick and easy deaths. Unwanted species of fish also die in the nets, and many of them are later thrown away as rubbish.

■ *What can you do?*

How do you feel about fish? Do you think they're cold, insensitive creatures? Do you care what happens to them?

If you eat fish now but want to change, you could eat less, substituting a vegetarian meal instead.

If you eat tuna, buy only tins with 'caught with pole and line' on the label. This means they have not been caught using drift nets.

See also AQUARIA, FISH FARMING, TROPICAL FISH.

Fish farming

Fish farming (or aquaculture) has been practised for centuries in the Far East, where fish, bred and kept for food, swim amongst the rice paddies. This system has never been as intensive as the new fish farms established in the lochs and fiords of Scotland and Norway. This fish farming is the equivalent of FACTORY FARMING in the fishing industry. Britain and Norway are the main countries farming fish on a large scale – mainly salmon and turbot, but there are plans to farm halibut and cod. The fish are grown in hatcheries before being transferred to huge floating cages in the sea or in lochs.

Fish farming may seem like free-range farming because the fish are in their element, water, but although they are in water they are confined along with thousands of others in a cage. Many fish, especially salmon, are migratory, and their life cycle involves swimming thousands of kilometres. Opponents say that caging them not only curbs their natural behaviour but also puts them under great stress because of overcrowding – their high disease rate may be linked to this. The diseases are controlled with chemicals in their water and feed. Chemicals are also fed to salmon to colour their flesh. Wild salmon have pink flesh, but when they are farmed it goes grey. There have been several health warnings about the effects of eating fish which have been treated with colouring chemicals.

Because fish farming is a relatively new industry, it is not certain how it affects the environment, although there is evidence of POLLUTION from the fish droppings and from chemical treatments in the water. Critics of the industry also say that fish-eating mammals such as seals and otters are often killed to protect fish stocks.

However, fish farming does produce cheaper fish on the supermarket shelf!

■ *What can you do?*

It's almost impossible to know which fish is farmed unless you're buying from the boat or from a trout farm. In shops, you can ask the fishmonger or supermarket manager, who may know the source of their fish supplies.

Think about what you eat – do you want to eat fish? Can you change your diet if you don't want to (see VEGETARIANS)?

Food fears

Over recent years, several 'food scares' have hit the headlines – salmonella poisoning in EGGS, listeria in soft cheeses and 'mad cow disease' possibly affecting beef. About 10,000 people suffer from food poisoning each week in Britain, and about 100 die of it each year. Many cases are related to meat or meat products.

Most food poisoning is caused by bacteria in food. Healthy bodies can cope with small amounts of these bacteria, but not with large amounts. Salmonella bacteria can be found in all animals, including humans. The bacteria are thought to be present in 80 per cent of frozen chickens. Campylobacter is also found in many chickens, and in some cooked meats. Both these bacteria are rarely found in vegetables or vegetarian dishes. Many cases of food poisoning are the result of bad housekeeping – if fridges are not kept cold enough, kitchens are dirty and food is old or badly kept, bacteria can grow rapidly.

The increase of salmonella-contaminated eggs was a major food scare in 1988 and resulted in a drop in egg sales and the destruction of infected flocks of hens. The cause of this salmonella infection was found: feeding battery hens on meal which contained ground-up slaughterhouse waste as well as 'recycled' dead chickens. Under natural conditions, hens are herbivores (they eat plants), but they were being forced to be carnivores and eat animals already infected with salmonella. The bacteria were passed on to the eggs.

BSE (bovine spongiform encephalopathy), or 'mad cow disease', is also thought to be caused by contaminated slaughterhouse products being fed to herbivores. BSE is a brain disease which affects cows. It is known to have killed over 27,000 cattle in Britain. In 1988 the Ministry of Agriculture ruled that infected cattle must be slaughtered and their carcasses destroyed, and in 1989 the brain, spinal cord and some other internal organs were banned from human food (they were used in meat pies, sausages, meat paste, etc.). The Ministry says that humans should not now eat infected meat. It can take years for the BSE symptoms to show in cattle, so it could still be possible for infected cattle to be slaughtered and butchered for meat.

With both salmonella and BSE, farmers and feed manufacturers disregarded the animals' natural diet in order to reduce costs by using up slaughterhouse waste. Many people blame the factory farming system for these outbreaks.

Other food fears include the use of the growth hormone BST in dairy cows: see MILK.

■ *What can you do?*

Do you know how to store and cook food properly? It is worth knowing, whether or not you eat meat. Foodline (the Food Safety Advisory Centre) can help you with advice and information.

Look at your own diet. What do you want to eat? Do you want to eat meat, or be VEGETARIAN? Can you buy free-range or organic food?

Read the 'What can you do?' sections on EGGS and FACTORY FARMING.

Food without cruelty

FACTORY FARMING, growth hormones, pesticides, food additives and colourings, agricultural POLLUTION and artificial fertilisers are just some of the reasons people choose to grow or eat organic.

Organic food is produced without the use of artificial pesticides and fertilisers. Fruit and vegetables are not the only food that can be organic; it is now possible to buy organic meat, milk and other dairy products. Animals on organic farms are not reared on factory farms but in traditional ways with respect for their natural behaviour, diet and well-being. They are not treated with drugs or chemicals, and their diet has to be 80 per cent organic too.

Free-range eggs and meat are another option – slightly different from organic. Here chickens, pigs and cattle have been allowed to wander freely in pastures for some of the time. However, the food they eat may not necessarily be organic.

Growing some of your own food is another way of ensuring the quality of your vegetables. It takes time and some money, but the results can be very satisfying. If you've got the space, keeping your own chickens can supply you with free-range eggs and help you to recycle waste food.

■ *What can you do?*

Look at your diet and think about whether you want to change it. Avoid processed and mass-produced foods. If possible, buy organic and free-range food. It's usually more expensive, but you know no artificial pesticides or chemicals have been used on it.

Many supermarkets and health food stores now stock organic and free-range food. If they don't, contact the manager and ask him or her if they will stock some items. See the section on LABELLING.

Even better – if it's possible and you're interested – grow your own. If you don't have a garden, you can rent an allotment – contact your local council for further information on allotments. Contact the Soil Association or Henry Doubleday Research Association for further information on organic food and gardening. WWOOF (Working Weekends on Organic Farms) have a scheme where you can work on an organic farm in exchange for bed and board.

There are several useful books to read: *The Kind Food Guide* by Audrey Eyton (Penguin, 1991); *The Organic Consumer Guide*, edited by David Mabey and Alan and Jackie Gear (Thorsons, 1990) and *Month-by-Month Organic Gardening* by Lawrence Hills (Thorsons, 1989).

Frogs' legs

Frogs' legs (or *les grenouilles*) are found on some restaurant menus, especially in French and Italian restaurants. Over recent years they have become more popular as a luxury food. As the European supply of frogs could not keep pace with demand, they have been imported from countries such as India, Bangladesh, Egypt and Indonesia. Each year about 300 million frogs are supplied to European and North American restaurants.

The frogs are 'hunted' from rice paddies by villagers. They are taken to cutting centres, where they are killed by being sliced in half alive. The legs are then packed in ice for export. The frogs' bodies are left to die, which can take up to an hour.

Apart from the cruelty involved, there are strong ecological reasons for not eating frogs' legs. The frogs eat insect pests and land crabs and in India, for example, the pest population grew rapidly as frogs were caught and exported in huge numbers. At one stage India was spending £13 million to import chemical pesticides to deal with the pest problem, while receiving only £5.5 million from the export of frogs' legs. Pesticides can poison other wildlife in the area and threaten human health. India has now banned the killing and export of frogs, but other Asian countries, particularly Indonesia, continue the trade.

■ *What can you do?*

Don't eat frogs' legs. You can write to the restaurant or shop concerned, asking them to stop selling frogs' legs and telling them why. Compassion in World Farming (CIWF) will also write to restaurants and shops if you supply names and addresses.

CIWF also run a public awareness campaign. They can supply you with a campaign kit of posters, stickers and leaflets which you can use to inform others.

Write to your MEP (Member of the European Parliament –

name and address from your public library) asking him or her to encourage a ban on the import of frogs' legs to European Community countries.

Fur

To make one fur coat it takes about 16–20 beavers, 130–200 chinchillas or 35–40 mink. Producing the furs to make into coats is not a pleasant business. It is estimated that 25 million animals are caught in the wild each year for their fur. The main trapping countries are the former Soviet Union, the United States and Canada, and the most sought-after animals are foxes, mink, racoons, beavers, lynx and other wild cats. The traps are totally indiscriminate – they catch any animal, whether it is wanted for fur or not. Many of these animals are caught in the leghold trap, which is notorious for the suffering and cruelty it inflicts on its victims (see TRAPPING).

Fur-bearing animals are also 'farmed', and about 45 million are raised this way each year. Mink and fox are the main farmed animals, and most of the farms are in Scandinavia and the Soviet Union. The farming of animals for fur raises similar questions to those on FACTORY FARMING for food. The animals are caged in small areas, denied anything like normal behaviour, space and social activity. They develop abnormal behaviour because of this. Fur farm animals are slaughtered by neck dislocation, gassing, poisoning or electrocution, and skinned while the body is warm to prevent the fur losing its quality.

Fur is a multi-million-dollar business worldwide, and there is a growing trade in many countries as well as a black-market trade in furs of ENDANGERED SPECIES. The fur traders defend their industry, maintaining that they help to control wild animal populations, although many zoologists say that animals have their own inbuilt population-control mechanisms.

For most people in the world, furs are luxury clothing. They are not necessary for survival, and plenty of alternative measures are available. They are worn as a symbol of wealth and glamour. In Britain, the good news on the fur trade is the success of anti-fur campaigns by organisations such as Lynx. They have mounted vigorous advertising campaigns with slogans such as 'It takes up to 40 dumb animals to make a fur coat. But only one to wear it.' They have succeeded in changing public opinion in Britain, so that now seven out of ten people think it is wrong to kill animals for their fur. Many fur shops, fur farms and fur traders have been forced out of business. Also, the European Community (EC) is to place a ban on fur from some animals caught in leghold traps. This will take effect from January 1995.

■ *What can you do?*

Don't wear furs, as coats, hats, gloves or trimmings. Also avoid furry toys made with real fur. Don't be tempted to wear fake furs either. They look real, and may put out the message that wearing fur is OK. Tell your family and friends too.

Lynx is the main organisation fighting the fur trade. You can support them by joining them or by purchasing their high-quality T-shirts or other merchandise. They also produce information sheets.

Write to your MP, asking him or her for their position on fur farms and asking for labelling of furs made from animals trapped in the wild.

Write to your MEP (Member of the European Parliament) asking him or her to support proposals for a ban on the import of furs to Europe.

If you have old furs you want to get rid of, send them to Lynx, who will destroy them.

Genetic engineering

Genetic engineering is a biological technique which takes genes from one species and introduces them into another. Genes are the blueprints for life: chemical messengers containing instructions on what we look like, and some behaviour patterns. Genes are passed on through generations, so offspring inherit certain characteristics, such as eye colour, from their parents.

By moving genes about, scientists have been able to increase crop yields, develop disease-resistant crops, speed up growth in animals and produce synthetic body substances such as insulin, which is used in treating diabetes. Genetic engineering is now a fast-growing industry with major multinational companies involved.

But many people are concerned about safety, animal welfare and moral issues. There are fears that inserting a 'foreign' gene into an animal is not predictable, and we do not know what the results will be. Already some experiments have caused animals to suffer. Pigs engineered to produce human growth hormone were infertile and suffered from arthritis. Also, if farm animals are genetically engineered, are their food products safe to eat? Does genetic engineering prop up the FACTORY FARMING industry, with animals engineered to be no more than meat machines?

However, genetic engineering has reduced the number of animals used in some processes. Rennet, used to make cheese, is taken from calves' stomachs. Rennet can now be made artificially by genetically engineering the rennet of only one calf. This means that fewer calves are used in cheese-making, although it is debatable whether this makes cheese completely free of slaughter-house products.

Another set of issues arises from genetically engineering animals to produce drugs or tissues for human medicine. For example, if genes for a blood-clotting protein needed by haemophiliacs are inserted into the eggs of a mouse, the mouse's offspring will produce milk high in these proteins. The mouse can then be used as a 'living factory' to produce drugs more cheaply than by more usual methods.

In the USA new genetic life forms have been patented or licensed as inventions, and this is also likely to happen in the European Community. The first patented animal was a mouse genetically engineered to develop cancer within ninety days of birth so that it could be used in testing anti-cancer drugs. Critics say that it debases living beings to patent them as inventions, and treats them as machines.

Genetic engineering does interfere with the natural life of animals, but this is nothing new in the human–animal relationship. Does it exploit animals? Are some benefits worth any suffering or stress in animals? Genetic engineering raises moral dilemmas about life. Is it morally right to interfere with or control nature by altering the very stuff of life? Are humans playing God, or just tinkering with the natural process of evolution?

■ *What can you do?*

The issues are difficult – so find out more and think about what you feel. You can get more information from the National Centre for Biotechnology Education and the Genetics Forum.

Try to get the issues discussed in school, college, youth club, church or other groups.

Hare coursing

At hare-coursing meetings, hares are usually hunted by two greyhounds, whippets or lurcher dogs. These dogs hunt by sight rather than smell, and the hares are driven by about thirty people, called beaters, within sight of the dogs. The dogs are then released, and they chase the hare until it escapes or is caught. The hare is killed when it is torn to pieces by the dogs or, if it is still alive when the handlers or 'pickers-up' arrive, it is killed by having its neck broken. A chase usually covers about half a mile and lasts about forty seconds. The meetings are run under strict National Coursing Club (NCC) rules, and judges award points for the speed and work of each dog. The NCC say that the object of coursing is to test greyhounds, not to kill hares, and that the rules of coursing are designed to favour hares.

About a thousand people in Britain take part in the organised sport, and many more watch and bet on which greyhound will win. Coursing takes place between September and March each year. There have been many attempts to ban coursing, but parliamentary Bills have always been overturned by the pro-coursing MPs. An opinion poll in 1990 showed that 85 per cent of British people disapproved of coursing.

Many hares are also coursed 'informally' in country fields as practice for dogs, as sport or as a pest-control measure.

■ *What can you do?*

Write to your MP, asking for his or her views on hare coursing and asking for a ban on this sport.

Find out more from the League Against Cruel Sports and the National Coursing Club.

See 'What can you do?' section under HUNTING.

Healthcare

Keeping yourself healthy feels good, looks good and is kinder to animals! Prevention is better than cure, and by keeping healthy, you use fewer drugs and medicines, so fewer MEDICAL EXPERIMENTS need to be performed. In Finland, deaths from heart disease dropped by 40 per cent after a five-year health-education campaign which persuaded people to change to a healthier diet.

Over the last twenty years many people have come to feel unhappy about conventional medicine, which is based on drug treatment or surgery, often because these treatments deal with the symptoms of the illness rather than its root cause. They have turned to alternative or complementary medicine.

Complementary medicine has a 'holistic' approach. This means that it considers the whole person – their mind, body, spirit, lifestyle and environment – in relation to their illness. It also aims to stimulate the body's ability to heal itself. Complementary medicine usually treats illness with natural plant products which do not require laboratory testing on animals and are often free of any animal product. Complementary therapies include herbalism, acupuncture, osteopathy, massage, homeopathy, flower remedies, yoga and relaxation, and many others.

Although many people swear by complementary therapies, their success has not been scientifically demonstrated and they face considerable opposition from the medical world. For this reason many people feel that they are best seen as a complement to conventional medicine rather than as an alternative.

■ *What can you do?*

Help yourself by taking responsibility for your own health. This might mean looking at your lifestyle, including diet, exercise, smoking, drinking and relaxation. If you take care of yourself, you may never need medical treatment. There are lots of good books on the subject, which you can borrow from your public library.

The British Union for the Abolition of Vivisection (BUAV) is running a campaign called 'Health with Humanity'. They are calling for an end to medical experiments on animals and a move towards prevention of illness rather than cure. A booklet explaining their campaign is available.

BUAV ask people to write to their MPs and to the Minister of Health asking them to support measures to ban animal experiments, direct resources into preventive healthcare and provide complementary medicine on the National Health Service.

The British Holistic Medical Association can provide you with further information on complementary medicine. The Health Education Authority also have a range of free leaflets on personal health.

Holidays

Going on holiday is usually an enjoyable experience – it's hard to see how animal welfare issues might be involved, but there are several things to watch out for.

In Spain, chimpanzees are used by beach photographers as 'props'. The photographers approach tourists at summer resorts such as Benidorm, offering to take their photo holding a chimp. It costs about £5 and the tourist ends up with a 'cute' photo souvenir. What most tourists don't know is how the chimps get to Spain.

They are captured from their wild African habitat by local hunters (see TRADE IN WILD ANIMALS). The mother is usually killed, as only the baby chimps are wanted. They are then sedated with drugs and exported (illegally) to Spain. The story gets worse . . . their teeth are often pulled out to stop them biting tourists, and when they grow too big (about five years old) and are no longer so appealing, they are killed, dumped or sold to research laboratories. There are also reports of lion cubs being used by beach photographers. These are dumped at an even earlier age.

Tourism is growing worldwide, especially as people in Western countries have more money and leisure time. They also have a taste for seeing sites of great natural beauty and unique wildlife habitats. But so many people now visit these places that the environment and its inhabitants, the wildlife, are being harmed. In Africa, tourists on safari want to see the 'famous' animals such as leopard and elephant. Some leopards and elephants spend much of their day being followed by safari vehicles, and their natural hunting behaviour is disturbed.

Concern about tourism has led to the growth of the 'eco-friendly tourism', which aims to reduce the impact of tourists on wild places, local people and wildlife, and some tour operators are already responding by changing tours to minimise damage to sensitive areas.

■ *What can you do?*

If you are on holiday in Spain, remember that beach photographers would not exist without tourists' money. Don't have your photo taken with any wild animal. Tell any people you are travelling with about the trade in wild animals.

If you are on a package holiday, complain to your tour operator and ask them to lobby the Spanish tourist authorities.

Complain to the Spanish Embassy, 24 Belgrave Square, London SW1 8QA, and the Spanish National Tourist Office, 57 St James's Street, London SW1A 1LD. If you have seen a photographer using wild animals, say when and where.

If you want to find an 'eco-friendly' holiday, a guidebook has been published called *The Good Tourist – A Worldwide Guide for the Green Traveller* (by Kate Wood and Syd House, Mandarin, 1991). Further information on green travel is available from International Green Flag.

If you're going on holiday, make sure your PETS are going to be looked after properly while you're away.

Don't buy souvenirs and curios made from wild animals – see ENDANGERED SPECIES. See also BIG GAME HUNTING, BULLFIGHTING.

Homes and gardens

Just about every product used around the house and garden is tested on animals. It's virtually impossible in our society *not* to use products that have been tested on animals or have animal ingredients.

Bleaches, polishes, washing-up liquid, washing powder, softener and disinfectants are all tested for toxicity, using the same tests as for COSMETICS AND TOILETRIES. In the garden, weedkillers and pesticides have been tested for toxicity and on the pests they're designed to kill.

Many of these products are also harmful to the environment, contributing to land and water POLLUTION.

■ *What can you do?*

More environment-friendly, cruelty-free and vegetarian/vegan household products are coming on to the market, and many can now be found in high-street supermarket chains. Check out the labels when you go shopping (see LABELLING). If they're not in your local supermarket or health shop, ask the shop manager if he or she will stock them.

Animal Aid and the RSPCA can supply you with a list of cruelty-free products and *The Cruelty-Free Shopper* by Lis Howlett (Bloomsbury, 1989) gives comprehensive listings.

Don't buy products labelled 'new' or 'improved' because they will have been newly tested on animals.

Use traditional, do-it-yourself cleaners such as water and vinegar to clean windows or soda crystals to remove grease. A useful guide is *Green Living: Practical Ways to Make Your Home Environment Friendly*, by Bernadette Vallely (Thorsons, 1991).

If you're into gardening, go organic – it's healthier and kinder to the environment and to animals. The Henry Doubleday Research Association or the Soil Association can give you advice and information on gardening without chemicals.

Horse racing

Horse racing is patronised by thousands of people, from royalty to Mr or Ms Public. It is also very big business, turning over millions of pounds a year. The stars of the show are the beautiful and superbly athletic racehorses. They are highly trained, well kept and well fed, so they are in prime condition on the day of the race. Many people feel that there is no better example of the partnership between humans and animals. However, there has been some disquiet about the racing world. Are the horses being exploited to make money? Are they quite as well treated as they appear?

Critics of racing say that the horses are trained too hard and too young. This puts them under great physical strain and can contribute to their early death through ill-health (often heart failure). When their racing days are over, many horses are destroyed even though they may not be very old.

Another criticism of racing is the use of the whip. Is it right to inflict pain to win races? There have been demands for a ban. Over the years there have also been calls to end races over difficult courses such as the Grand National. In this famous – or infamous – race, horses regularly have to be destroyed after falling at enormous fences.

■ *What can you do?*

Don't support horse racing by going to the races or by having a bet.

If you see races on television or at the racetrack where horses appear to be mistreated (such as excessive whipping), write to the Jockey Club and complain. Give them full details of time, place, name of horse and jockey. If you see the incident on television, you can also complain to the television company showing the race.

Hunting

Hunting includes SHOOTING, TRAPPING, and hunting with packs of dogs. In Britain, it is considered by some a traditional country sport and by others a BLOOD SPORT. Packs of dogs or hounds are used for hunting foxes, deer, hare and mink.

Fox-hunting: The night before the hunt, the foxes' burrows (earths) are blocked up to stop them returning there. When a fox is scented by the hounds, it is pursued by the hunt until it is lost or killed by the dogs. Each year about 20,000 foxes are killed by the 186 packs of hounds in Britain.

Deer-hunting: In Britain this is confined to three West Country packs. It is similar to fox-hunting, but the strength of the deer (often a stag) usually means a longer chase. After the chase the exhausted deer is cornered by hounds, and shot when the hunt riders arrive. However, it may be attacked by hounds before the riders reach it. After the kill, the deer is cut up and the landowners and hunt supporters receive the meat. The hounds are given the entrails.

Hare-hunting: There are about a hundred hare-hunting packs of dogs (usually beagles, bassets or harriers). The harriers are followed by horseriders and the beagle and basset packs by people on foot. The hare is chased until it escapes or is killed by the pack.

Hunters say that hunting is an effective method of controlling pest animals, such as foxes which prey on chickens and lambs, and deer which damage forest plantations and crops. They also say that the landscape and its wildlife are conserved because landowners keep wildlife areas for hunt animals to breed. More-over, they argue that country sports are a tradition and provide employment in the countryside. They defend their right to kill, saying that they have as much right to hunt as any other animal does, and that the animal at least has a sporting chance. Some hunters honestly admit that they hunt because they enjoy it.

Anti-hunting groups say that hunting is neither humane nor efficient but simply cruel and barbaric. The fox, deer, mink or hare is subjected to an exhausting and terrifying ordeal which often results in its violent death. They argue that hunting does little to control pests or conserve the landscape. They also point out that 15,000 hounds are destroyed each year when they are no longer fit enough for hunting. As an acceptable alternative they promote drag-hunting, where an artificial scent is laid.

■ *What can you do?*

Hunting is opposed by many animal organisations, specifically the Hunt Saboteurs Association and League Against Cruel Sports. You can support them and get more information from them. If you want to know more about the pro-hunting case, contact the British Field Sports Society.

Over a hundred local councils have banned hunting on their land. You can write to your own council to see what their position is. If they don't have a ban, you can write outlining why you think they should. You can also write to private landowners in your area, asking them not to allow hunting on their land.

The Hunt Saboteurs Association actively attempt to stop hunts, using 'non-violent direct action tactics' such as confusing the hounds with scents and sounds. If you want to become an active member, think very carefully about what it entails and be aware that there have been violent incidents between hunters and hunt saboteurs. There is a youth section called Fox Cubs which aims to inform, educate and campaign against blood sports.

See also HARE COURSING, PEST CONTROL.

Information

Good up-to-date information is important. Without it, you literally don't know what you're talking about. If you want to be taken seriously when you talk or write about what you believe, educate yourself about the issues. Don't just confirm what you already know, or think you know – find out the views of scientists, farmers or drug companies as well as animal rights campaigners.

■ *What can you do?*

There are lots of ways you can find out more about animal rights and animal welfare.

Read about it. There's a reading list at the end of this book, and you can get the books from your local public library, school or college library or, if you want to buy any of them, from a bookshop. Newspapers and magazines often have articles and news reports and are a good way of keeping up to date.

Health food shops and natural beauty shops, such as The Body Shop, frequently have leaflets you can take and sometimes a selection of booklets to buy.

Nearly all the animal organisations listed in this book have magazines and newsletters as well as information leaflets. Some are free; others are priced. Contact the organisation you're interested in for details.

Listen and watch. Television and radio are also good sources of information. The news often has stories on animal campaigns, and the many wildlife programmes often look at environmental issues. Animal issues turn up on all sorts of programmes, so it's largely a question of keeping your eyes and ears open.

Meetings. You can learn a lot from listening and talking to other people. Animal organisations occasionally hold meetings, workshops and conferences you can go to. Some are national meetings, while others are run by local groups. Contact the organisations which interest you for further details.

You could also organise your own discussion groups at school, college, youth club, or wherever. Hearing other people's point of view can be interesting and often entertaining. Many organisations will provide a speaker for lectures and groups – again, contact the organisation which interests you. Consider having a debate with speakers putting forward opposing points of view so that you can hear different arguments.

Joining groups

If you want to be more involved in the animal rights and welfare movement, you can join an organisation or group. There are lots of organisations to choose from, depending on your area of interest – see the directory at the end of this book.

Organisations can provide information through leaflets, magazines and meetings; they may also campaign through demonstrations, petitions and marches. Many also sell attractive T-shirts, badges and other goodies.

Some organisations have youth sections or special youth groups. These are:

Animal Aid Youth Group
The Animals' Defenders (National Anti-Vivisection Society)
Earth Action (Friends of the Earth)
Farm Watch (Compassion in World Farming)
Fox Cubs (Hunt Saboteurs Association)
RSPCA Junior Membership
The Vegetarian Society Youth Group
WATCH (Royal Society for Nature Conservation)
Youth Ornithologists' Club (Royal Society for the Protection of Birds)
Young People's Trust for Endangered Species

Many other groups have a reduced membership fee for young people.

■ *What can you do?*

Write to the groups that interest you for further details and costs of joining. If you want to get involved locally, ask for the name and address of your local group organiser.

If you already belong to a group such as Scouts, Guides, a youth club, church group, or any other group, you could bring up animal issues when you have discussions.

You can set up your own group. Many of the biggest and most successful groups were started by one or two people who believed in their cause.

Kinship

Kinship is a word used to describe a relationship between people in societies, whether it is a blood relationship (such as between parents and children) or some other relationship. It is the sense of recognising someone as 'kin' or family. In a wider sense, many people feel kinship or a connection with other animals. This quote is from the famous psychologist C. G. Jung:

> Because they are so closely akin to us . . . I loved all warm-blooded animals, who have souls like ourselves and with whom, so I thought, we have an instinctive understanding. We experience joy and sorrow, love and hate, hunger, thirst, fear and trust in common . . .

Animals have similar features to people. They have eyes, ears, limbs and noses. A lot of their behaviour is like ours. They play, find a mate, have babies, feel pain. These similarities shouldn't be a big surprise because we are all related through evolution. It may be millions of years ago that we became different species, but we all evolved from the same source. Animals are our relatives. This may be why many people feel kinship with them.

Many people forget or don't know that humans are animals too, and they consider other animals to be inferior. Often, comparison to an animal is a common form of abuse or condemnation. How many times have you heard 'they behaved like animals' or 'ignorant pig'?

The relationship between humans and other animals is complex. We have lived on the earth together for millions of years, and humans have used animals for food, clothing, gods, currency, companionship, entertainment, trade, tools, and for many other purposes. We love, hate, pamper, exploit and abuse them.

■ *What can you do?*

Consider how you feel about animals – do you feel a sense of kinship with them? Do you feel differently about a dog and a spider, or a whale and an ant? Do you know why?

Keep your eyes open for examples of 'they behaved like animals' remarks. If you see them in newspapers you can write to the editor pointing out that most animals don't behave as badly as humans, and that humans are animals too!

See also DIFFERENT CULTURES, DIFFERENT OPINIONS and SPECIESISM.

Labelling

If we were aware that our food was factory-farmed or our cosmetics were tested on animals before we bought them, would it make a difference? The evidence is that it would. Sales of free-range eggs are on the increase, and cruelty-free cosmetics shops like The Body Shop continue to make good profits. But so far only a tiny minority of the products we buy have labelling relating to animal welfare. The situation is complicated by the many different wordings that can be found on different products.

Labelling could cover many more areas than it does now. Is that bacon from a pig that has spent its life in a stall or in a field? Is any of the product produced through GENETIC ENGINEERING? Is it tested on animals? Was the animal killed by RELIGIOUS SLAUGH-TER methods?

The RSPCA would like to see labelling of products extended and standardised so that consumers know exactly what they are buying. They are working on a standards scheme for food produced by humane methods. Farmers and producers who meet the RSPCA's welfare standards will be allowed to state this on the product label. At the time of writing, the scheme is not yet in operation, but keep your eyes open for these labels, which will start appearing soon.

There is some animal welfare labelling you can look out for.

Cosmetics

Cruelty-free implies that the product contains no animal ingredients, and neither the product nor the ingredients have been tested on animals.

Not tested on animals means that this particular formulation will not have been tested on animals. However, the original ingredients might have been.

We do not test our products on animals means that the company itself does not test on animals. However, testing might be done for them by another company.

Many products claim to be cruelty-free, but it's almost impossible to check this and there have been cases of dishonesty by manufacturers using cruelty-free labelling as a marketing ploy.

The only certain way to make sure cosmetics are cruelty-free is to buy products marked with the British Union for the Abolition of Vivisection (BUAV) 'white rabbit' logo, or listed in the approved product guide (see 'What can you do?' section below).

Food

Food labels have to tell you certain information such as what you are buying, quantity, ingredients (including additives) and nutritional value, sell-by or use-by date, and so on. Other wordings to look out for:

Suitable for vegetarians means that the food contains no slaughterhouse products such as meat, fish or animal fat. It may contain dairy products. The label may also display a V symbol.

Organic means that the food is produced without the use of pesticides or artificial fertilisers. For meat to be organic the animal must be fed on a diet that is at least 80 per cent organically produced. Drugs, medications, growth hormones and additives cannot be administered to the animals.

The UK Register of Organic Food Standards (UKROFS) has been set up by the government to regulate organic standards. The Soil Association is the other main organisation which sets organic standards. You may see either of their logos on organic food.

Free-range means that animals must have continuous daytime access to open-air pens or pasture; however, the pasture itself does not have to be organic. Each laying hen must have at least 10 square metres of space. Farms which come up to the standards of the Free-Range Egg Association (FREGG) have a blue triangle logo on their egg boxes. FREGG can supply you with information on other types of egg labelling, such as 'barn-laid' or 'perchery' eggs.

Conservation Grade is often found on cereals and some meat. It means it is produced under the Guild of Conservation Food Producers' regulations. It is not organic, as some chemical weedkillers and additives may be used, but these chemicals will be only ones that break down easily in the soil and do not contaminate food. Animals must be kept in good conditions and some medications may be used on them when necessary.

Traditional, country fresh or farm fresh means nothing. Products may be marketed under these names to make you think they are free-range or organic.

'Caught with pole and line' on cans of tuna means that the fish are *not* caught with nets which can entangle DOLPHINS and other sea mammals.

■ *What can you do?*

Look carefully at labels when you're shopping. What you buy can make a difference, and consumers have real power.

If you're not happy or clear about what you read on a label, you can write to the manufacturer (their name and address should always be on the label) asking them what their procedures or ingredients are. You can also ask them to explain their policy on animal welfare.

Use the approved products guide produced by the RSPCA, British Union for the Abolition of Vivisection or Animal Aid. Other good guides are *The Cruelty-Free Shopper*, *The Organic Consumer Guide*, and *The Green Consumer Guide* (see book list for details).

Leather

Leather and suede are by-products of the SLAUGHTER industry. There is a plentiful supply because huge numbers of animals are killed for their meat. Leather is used for almost all shoes as well as many items of clothing, belts and straps, handbags, wallets, and for some furniture.

Many vegetarians and vegans avoid wearing leather because it is directly involved in the killing of animals. However, it is difficult to find alternatives for certain products such as shoes and boots in the usual high-street stores.

Leather is also treated with chemicals tested on animals.

■ *What can you do?*

It's up to you whether you decide to have leather products or not. If you want to ban leather from your life, there are more and more synthetic or fabric goods such as handbags and wallets available.

Footwear is probably the most difficult item to replace. Canvas shoes or trainers (without leather trimmings) are a good alternative, and there are now attractive Gore-tex walking boots and shoes on the market in outdoor shops.

Animal Aid, in association with Mocatan Ltd, offer some fashionable leather-look shoes, belts and jackets suitable for those who don't wish to wear slaughterhouse products. Contact Animal Aid for further details.

The Campaign Against Leather and Fur (CALF) can also help you with further information.

Litter

You wouldn't think a yoghurt pot was a potential killer, but if you're a hungry hedgehog, it could be. Food pots and containers, bottles and plastic wrappers have all proved to be death-traps for wild animals.

Dead hedgehogs have been found unable to free themselves from plastic containers, where they went looking for scraps of food, and small mammals have been found trapped in bottles and pots. Plastic is one of the most lethal litter killers because most of it is not biodegradable (it doesn't decompose). Plastic litter can be swallowed by animals, causing death or injury; it can also entangle them. Many birds, especially seabirds, have been found with plastic beer-can pack-holders round their necks. Fish, dolphins and seals have also been injured and killed by waste thrown into the sea.

Discarded and lost fishing tackle is another litter hazard on river banks and in the water. Water birds can become entangled in line and pierced with hooks.

Apart from the direct deaths caused by litter, it doesn't do the ENVIRONMENT a lot of good either. It looks ugly and contributes to POLLUTION problems.

■ *What can you do?*

If you're outside and you want to throw some litter away, either find a litter bin or take it home.

Make sure your dustbin has a heavy lid to stop hungry animals having a look inside.

Try to reduce the amount of litter and waste you create. Here are a few suggestions:

- refuse extra plastic bags in shops – take your own bag when you go shopping;
- avoid using disposable products; think about reusing or repairing things rather than throwing them away;
- recycle what you can – many local councils and supermarkets now have glass, paper and can recycling schemes.

Pick up any dangerous litter you see and put it in a bin. Remember to wash your hands afterwards or wear rubber gloves!

If you live near a river, canal, beach or lake that is used for fishing, you can patrol the banks and remove lost or discarded fishing tackle. The Campaign for the Abolition of Angling have an information sheet on angling litter.

The Tidy Britain Group specialises in all things to do with litter and waste. They have local groups you can join, information leaflets, and videos and educational packs for sale.

Markets

Between being raised on a farm and being slaughtered, most animals will, at some time, go to market to be sold. Markets are usually held in towns, and from there the animals may be sold to another farmer or to a butcher or meat wholesaler. If they're sold for SLAUGHTER they will usually go straight from the market to the abattoir.

Markets can be stressful and frightening places for animals. First, they have to be transported to the market by lorry (see TRANSPORT OF LIVE ANIMALS). Once there they may be handled carelessly or even cruelly. Sticks and electric goads may be used to make animals move, and they may be overcrowded in pens. There has been particular criticism of the repeated selling of young calves, with cases of calves only a few days old going to market and no restrictions on how many times they might go.

In 1991 new rules were brought in to improve the welfare of animals at markets. They make it an offence to cause or permit any injury or unnecessary suffering to an animal; restrict the use of sticks and goads; and give minimum standards for handling, feeding and watering, caging and bedding. The rules also say that calves under twelve weeks old may not be marketed more than twice in a twenty-eight-day period. Market operators are required to appoint a member of staff to attend to animal welfare.

■ *What can you do?*

If you go to a market and see anything you consider to be cruel and causing suffering, you should report it immediately to the market's appointed welfare officer. He or she should be identifiable by a badge or armband. Alternatively, the market auctioneers should know who is responsible for welfare. Markets are required to display a notice giving details of how to contact local-authority inspectors and the government's veterinary officer, and you can report the incident to them or the RSPCA if you get no response from the welfare officer.

Compassion in World Farming and the RSPCA both work to improve the welfare of animals at market. You can find out more from them and support their campaigns.

Medical experiments

People may think it is wrong to test COSMETICS AND TOILETRIES or weapons (see WARFARE) on animals, but when it comes to medicines or operations, the arguments become more difficult because human health is in question. Most of us have at some time used medicines, had vaccinations or anaesthetic, all of which will have been tested on animals. So we are all involved in this issue, not just the research scientists who perform the tests.

Many diseases and illnesses affect us, and in our society most are treated with medicines or drugs, or by surgery. Today, people live longer than they've ever done. However, the most important causes of better health over the last hundred years have been better hygiene (clean water and sewage management), improved housing and diet.

Developing and manufacturing drugs is a billion-dollar business, and it is very competitive. There is a long period of research before drugs are allowed to be used on patients. The research looks at how animal bodies work, what happens in illness, and how they respond to various drugs. All chemicals used on humans have to be screened for safety and effectiveness. This is usually done by testing them on animals. In Britain in 1989, 289,716 animals were used in medical experiments in drug company laboratories, universities and polytechnics, hospitals and government research departments.

The main arguments put forward by people who support the use of animals in medical experiments are:

- the benefits to humans outweigh the suffering to animals;
- experiments are strictly controlled and animals are well cared for, with pain and distress kept to an absolute minimum;
- thousands of people would not be alive today without modern drugs and surgery developed through animal experiments;
- animal tests are essential to developing new drugs, medicines and surgical techniques;
- many animals benefit from the tests, as the drugs or techniques are later used by vets.

Opponents of animal testing say:

- experiments inflict terrible pain and suffering on animals, and it is morally wrong to do this;
- experiments tell us about the effects of drugs on animals, not on humans. As a result, the tests can be misleading – for example, many drugs such as Thalidomide and Opren were tested on animals but had disastrous side-effects when given to people;
- many experiments are totally unnecessary, as they are just testing different versions of the same drug (these are known as 'me-too' drugs and are usually marketed under a different name but offer no great improvement to drugs already on the market);
- animal testing is based on the belief that modern science can cure all our ills and animal research is the only method of testing medicine and surgery.

Is animal suffering the price we must pay for saving human lives or improving human health? Do we have a right to protect our own species at the expense of other species? Medical experimentation is one of the most difficult and emotional areas of animal rights questions. It makes us look at our BELIEFS and EMOTIONS.

It can be very difficult to argue against experimentation when a relative or friend is ill. If you are faced with the question 'Would you let a baby die because you won't test a drug or operation on a mouse?' the emotional pressure on you to come down in favour of testing is overwhelming. But the arguments aren't as black-and-white as this, and maybe we don't have to make these agonising choices. Animal welfare organisations are calling for more money, skills and resources to be spent on safer and more humane ALTERNATIVES TO ANIMAL EXPERIMENTS and on building up a system of preventive HEALTHCARE. Maybe a gentler, more humane future lies in this direction.

■ *What can you do?*

Think about how you feel about this difficult issue. Do you think human need outweighs animal suffering?

Find out more. There are lots of organisations that can help you with further information: Animal Aid, Animals in Medicines Research Information Centre (AMRIC), British Union for the Abolition of Vivisection (BUAV), Dr Hadwen Trust for Humane Research, Fund for the Replacement of Animals in Medical Experiments (FRAME), National Anti-Vivisection Society, Research Defence Society (RDS), Royal Society for the Prevention of Cruelty to Animals (RSPCA).

Avoid taking new medicines and remedies and use only tried and tested ones. Look at your lifestyle and work towards making it healthier. If you are healthy, fewer drugs, less surgery and ultimately fewer animals will be used in research. BUAV is running a 'Health with Humanity' campaign – see HEALTHCARE.

Some medical charities sponsor research involving animal experiments, and you may not want to support these charities. Disabled Against Animal Research and Exploitation and the BUAV publish lists of charities which do and do not fund animal experiments.

See also ALTERNATIVES TO ANIMAL EXPERIMENTS, PRIMATES, VIVISECTION.

Migrating birds

Each year, birds migrating between Africa and Northern Europe have to run the gauntlet of hunters in Southern Europe. It is nothing short of mass slaughter, with up to 900 million birds killed by SHOOTING and TRAPPING each year – about 15 per cent of all migrating birds.

The hunting is done mainly in France, Spain, Italy, Malta, Greece and Cyprus, where hunting is a tradition. It may be a traditional sport, but the methods used are definitely hi-tech. Many of today's hunters are aided by four-wheel-drive vehicles, satellite weather forecasts, new roads and powerful and easy-to-use weapons. Anything that flies is fair game, and hunters will take even the tiniest birds such as goldfinches. The birds may be eaten in dishes such as blackbird pâté, or just hunted for fun.

In Italy alone, 100–250 million birds are killed each year. On the island of Sicily, it is their traditional belief that if a man shoots a honey buzzard his wife will be faithful to him. Consequently, thousands of migrating buzzards are shot each year to be stuffed and displayed as a symbol of manhood. The island of Malta is another offender. Shooting is a national sport, and anything that moves is shot. As a result there is very little wildlife left on the island, and hunters rely on migrating birds for their 'sport'.

Hunters see attempts by European animal welfare and bird protection groups to curb the scale of killing as a threat to their heritage. However, there are European Community (EC) directives to protect wild birds and regulate the numbers killed, protect habitats and outlaw large-scale or non-selective killing of birds (such as in traps). Much of the killing that goes on is illegal, but hunting laws are notoriously difficult to enforce. There is a very strong hunting lobby, backed by the gun and ammunition manufacturers.

■ *What can you do?*

Support the campaigns of the Royal Society for the Protection of Birds (RSPB) and the International Council for Bird Preservation (ICBP). Both are campaigning in Europe, and running conservation and education programmes in Southern Europe. They can also provide you with further information.

Animal welfare and bird protection organisations are asking tourists to boycott Malta. If you're planning to go there, or to any of the other offending countries, think about the issues involved. You may not want to cancel your trip, but you can do your own bit of education by talking to other people on the trip about the situation.

Write to your MP, MEP (Member of the European Parliament), the Secretary of State for the Environment and the President of the European Commission, asking them what they are doing to halt the illegal killing of birds in Europe.

Milk

Milk is a nourishing, wholesome and cheap food produced by contented cows grazing in country fields. Or is it? This is the image the milk adverts project, but the situation is not quite so rosy.

To produce cheap, plentiful supplies of milk, dairy cows are put under considerable stress. They are super-bred for the highest possible milk yield. To quote one professor of animal husbandry, Dr John Webster, the modern dairy cow has 'been genetically selected to be a high-performance machine, as highly tuned as a racing car . . . and like a car that's been pushed flat out . . . it goes bust more easily'. The high-performance cow, say animal welfare groups, is prone to illness through exhaustion, and is destroyed once she is past her peak.

Farmers disagree with this, saying that modern dairy farming does not put too much strain on the cows. However, organically reared cattle produce milk for longer, and on average their lives are twice as long, but they produce less milk.

BST

Another milk issue is BST. All cows produce a growth hormone naturally; it is called bovine somatotrophin, or BST. Scientists working in GENETIC ENGINEERING have developed a technique to produce BST artificially. Injecting it into dairy cows in small doses increases the amount of milk they produce. This is obviously of interest to farmers, because they can produce more milk from the same number of cows and increase profits. BST is heavily promoted by the drug companies who manufacture it.

There has been a lot of concern over the use of BST. Most of it centres on whether the milk is safe to drink. It appears that there are no short-term effects from drinking BST-treated milk, but no one knows the long-term effects on cows or humans.

Another issue in the BST story is that Europe already over-produces milk. Is there any need to increase production?

■ *What can you do?*

How much milk do you drink? Do you want to change this? There are milk substitutes, such as soya milk, which you can find in health food shops. Remember that milk is also used to make butter, cream, yoghurt, cheese, chocolate, ice cream and many other products. Look at the section on VEGANS if you are interested in giving it up altogether.

A few supermarket chains sell organic milk. This means that the cows graze on land which is not treated with artificial chemicals or pesticides, and will not have been chemically treated themselves. Organic milk is more expensive than ordinary milk.

Compassion in World Farming campaign for farm animal welfare and are monitoring the BST situation. They have a membership scheme, information sheets and a magazine, *Agscene*.

The Milk Marketing Board can also provide you with information on milk.

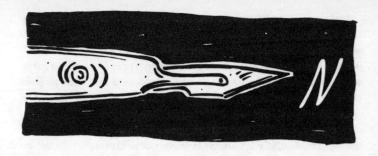

Neutering

Neutering means sterilising pet animals, usually cats and dogs, so that they can't breed. Male animals are castrated (their testicles are removed) and females are spayed (their womb and ovaries are removed).

Some people have their PETS neutered; others don't – some because they never even consider it, or don't until after puppies or kittens appear; others because they fear that an operation will harm their pet and believe that neutered pets are less healthy, fatter and lazier than un-neutered animals. Many people also feel that it is cruel and wrong to deprive animals of the right to reproduce. There is also resistance to neutering because humans easily identify with their pet animals. Neutering may arouse male fears of castration, and women may feel that all females should have a right to have babies.

Neutering doesn't rob animals of their life or vigour, but it does change their natural behaviour – for a start, they can't breed. Males are less likely to go wandering in search of a mate or spray urine to mark their territory. Females don't go on heat. There is a slight risk of harm with any operation, whether for humans or animals, but it's very small. Some people think that these changes in animal behaviour make domestic pets easier to live with. The fat and lazy neutered pet is a myth – there's no need for neutered pets to become overweight if they are fed and exercised properly. However, they usually need less food than un-neutered animals because they don't burn up so many calories.

How you feel about denying animals reproduction is your choice, but another element in the equation is the enormous overpopulation of pet animals. There are about 500,000 stray dogs in Britain, and thousands more animals are abandoned each week as their owners tire of them, or as unwanted kittens and puppies are got rid of. Animal rescue homes are full of dogs and cats in need of homes. The RSPCA kill 1,000 healthy dogs every day because homes cannot be found for them. This is probably the most compelling argument in favour of neutering.

■ *What can you do?*

If you have a pet which is not neutered, consider if you want to have it neutered. If you don't and it does have litters, can you find them all good homes? If you have a male animal you won't have this problem yourself, but someone who owns a female cat or dog might!

If you want to get a pet, contact the local animal rescue home. They usually have all shapes, sizes and ages to choose from, and you'll know you are helping reduce the number of animals destroyed each year.

Non-furry animals

It's easy to *ooh* and *aah* about furry animals, especially appealing and cuddly baby ones like kittens, koala bears and pandas. But what about the not-so-attractive animals such as snakes, spiders, cockroaches, slugs, rats and wasps? How much interest is there in their fate?

Most of these animals get only bad publicity. They are used extensively for their 'squirm factor' in films, where they are usually exterminated by heroes like Indiana Jones. The widespread revulsion to animals like these is nothing short of prejudice based on myths and misconceptions. All these animals have an important ecological role in the world – they may be waste-management experts efficiently clearing up the remains of dead plants and animals, plant pollinators or living pest controllers.

They rarely attack humans, usually only when provoked or in a life-threatening situation. They are not slimy, creepy, crawly or ugly. The real revulsion in this story should be reserved for what humans do to them!

Spiders, wasps, slugs, ants and many other insects are routinely squashed, poisoned and sprayed with insecticide for daring to enter a house or garden where they are doing no harm at all (and probably doing a lot for the local ecology). Lobsters and crabs are boiled alive before being served up in a restaurant. Reptiles such as snakes and crocodiles are persecuted throughout the world (see REPTILES).

Consider your own attitude to slugs, wasps and other non-furry animals. Do you find them revolting or fascinating? Which insects would you kill if they were in the house? Why?

■ *What can you do?*

How much do you know about non-furry animals? You can find out more from books (try the public library) and television and radio programmes. The Royal Entomological Society (RES), the Amateur Entomologists Society and the British Tarantula Society are the main organisations concerned with insects.

Don't kill insects in the house unless you're infested (see PEST CONTROL). You can collect them by trapping them in a jam jar while they're on the windowpane or a flat surface, then sliding a piece of paper or card under the rim of the jar to provide a lid. You can then release them outside. Spiders are useful household guests because they are a natural, non-pesticide flytrap!

Do you eat lobsters, crab or other shellfish, whether fresh or in fish products? Do you want to change what you eat?

Pâté de foie gras

Pâté de foie gras is a luxury food, mainly produced in France. It is a meat paste made from goose livers, and it is produced by force-feeding geese to enlarge the liver. The translation of 'pâté de foie gras' is 'pâté from crammed livers'.

In France, 2 million geese are force-fed each year. The process starts when the birds are about four months old and lasts for about four weeks. During this period the goose increases in weight by 61 per cent and the liver enlarges by 371 per cent. The birds are caged because any exercise would use up liver fat. To be 'crammed' the bird is restrained with its head raised so that the throat is open. Then mash is forced into the throat by a funnel tube. Sometimes an elastic band is placed around the bird's neck to stop it vomiting up the food. The birds are given increasing amounts of mash. In the final stages they receive over 1,300 g (2.5 lb) a day. This has been estimated as the equivalent of a human being fed 12 kilos (28 lb) of spaghetti a day.

This practice would be illegal in Britain because of our animal welfare laws, but it has not been banned in the rest of the European Community. Britain also continues to allow imports of pâté de foie gras, thereby supporting the industry abroad.

■ *What can you do?*

Think seriously about whether you want to eat pâté de foie gras. Many people just don't know how it is made, so tell other people about the production methods involved.

You can write to shop and restaurant owners selling pâté de foie gras, pointing out the cruelty to birds in this process.

Compassion in World Farming is campaigning against the production of pâté de foie gras, and they are asking people to write to their MPs requesting that imports to Britain should be banned. They also ask people to write to their MEP (Member of the European Parliament) calling for a ban on production in Europe. They produce leaflets you can distribute to restaurants and shops.

Perfume and aftershave

Expensive perfumes often have exotic, musky scents heavily promoted by the perfume companies as sexy and desirable. The musk scent is attractive to humans – which might seem strange, because it is secreted by the male musk deer! The musk is collected from a pod or sac which hangs next to the deer's genitals, then dried and ground into the musk grains used in perfume. Musk is so expensive (it is worth more than gold) that it is used only in the most expensive perfumes, usually those from French fashion houses. Musk deer are found only in Asia and parts of Siberia. The Chinese farm herds of these deer and have developed a technique to extract the musk without killing them. However, large amounts of musk are taken from wild deer, which are killed for this precious scent. Britain bans the import of musk because musk deer are an ENDANGERED SPECIES, but perfumes containing it are not banned.

Other perfume ingredients are civet, which is 'milked' from the anal gland of the Ethiopian civet, a member of the cat family, and castoreum, which is obtained from the scent glands of beavers. Beavers are not caught for their fur so much these days, so castoreum is in short supply.

An artificial musk scent has been manufactured, and this is usually used in cheaper perfumes.

Almost all perfumes will be tested on animals for safety to humans.

■ *What can you do?*

It is impossible to know from the bottle labels or packaging which perfumes use animal scents and which use synthetic scents. The only reliable non-animal perfumes are those produced by The Body Shop, Beauty Without Cruelty and other cruelty-free manufacturers (listed in *The Cruelty-Free Shopper* by Lis Howlett, Bloomsbury, 1989).

Write to perfume manufacturers and ask them:

- How do they obtain their ingredients, and do any ingredients contain animal products?
- How are these ingredients tested? Are they tested on animals in the UK or any other country by the company, its suppliers or a third party?

Pest control

Pests are animals which cause a nuisance. You may know plenty of them personally, but pests usually means plagues of insects, birds or mammals which destroy crops, livestock or property. In Britain, most farmers consider rabbits, rats, deer, pigeons and numerous insect species to be pests. Overseas, pests can be locusts, toads, mice, kangaroos, or a variety of other animals. In homes, we think of ants, cockroaches, wasps, woodlice and suchlike as pests.

Whether or not certain species are pests, and the measures used to control them, are matters of debate. Hunters maintain that HUNTING is a way of controlling pests such as foxes, but many conservationists say that foxes help farmers by eating other pests such as rabbits and voles. Pest animals can also be killed by SHOOTING, TRAPPING, ferrets, dogs and gassing. Poisoning is used by some farmers, even though it is illegal. Poison kills anything that eats it and is responsible for the deaths of many birds of prey such as eagles and buzzards.

Insect pests are usually killed by chemical pesticides, whether on the farm or in the house. Modern pesticides are sophisticated chemical mixtures – some kill only 'target' pests and leave others alive. But there is concern about pesticides being absorbed into fruit and vegetables and seeping into the soil and groundwater, eventually ending up in streams and rivers. The World Health Organisation estimate that one million people worldwide become ill through pesticide poisoning each year.

It may seem cruel to exterminate animals on such a scale, but how do you prevent large-scale damage by pests? What methods of killing are acceptable? Hunting may involve enjoyment and pleasure; pesticides can cause environmental and health problems.

■ *What can you do?*

Try not to use chemical pesticides in your home and garden. Learn to live with the insects in your home. Most are completely harmless and don't need to be killed unless you've got an infestation. You can also encourage their predators – for example, ladybirds will eat aphids and spiders' webs catch flies. There are organic pesticides available which do not damage the environment. The Henry Doubleday Research Association have information on these.

If you have mice or rats you want to get rid of, use a humane trap (one that catches the animal but does not kill it). You can then release the animal in the countryside or a park. You can buy these traps in pet shops. Also, find out how the animals are coming into the building and block up any holes or cracks. A cat is another good non-chemical, organic rodent-catcher.

If the infestation of any pest is severe, the environmental health department of the local council or a private pest-control company can be brought in to deal with it.

Pets

'Animals are such agreeable friends – they ask no questions, they pass no criticisms.' Is this why pets are so popular? The writer George Eliot, along with countless other humans over the centuries, obviously enjoyed their company. In Britain today there are 7.3 million dogs and 6.7 million cats, as well as millions of pet birds, guinea pigs, hamsters, rabbits, mice and TROPICAL FISH.

Very often the relationship between humans and their pet or companion animal benefits both parties. Pets have a safe and often luxurious lifestyle. Food is provided and usually some freedom to move about, scratch, sniff and meet others of their species. Their human owners have companionship, entertainment and, in some cases, protection. They can display their affection, their need to touch and stroke, their maternal or paternal feelings for a pet when perhaps they cannot do this to another human. Research has shown that people who have pets are less stressed and live longer than those who don't.

Unfortunately, humans can also abuse this relationship with pets by overfeeding, neglect or downright cruelty. In 1990, the RSPCA reported record levels of convictions for cruelty-to-animal offences. Dogs were the most abused animal, followed by horses and cats. Many pets are also abandoned when they are no longer wanted. Approximately 1,000 unwanted dogs are destroyed in Britain every week.

Huge amounts of money are spent on pet food. What many pet owners don't realise is that tinned pet meat is made from 'slaughterhouse waste' – all the bits of animals humans won't eat such as feet, ears, tails, internal organs. If you are a VEGETARIAN for moral reasons and also keep pets, you may find this difficult to handle. Dogs can exist on a well-balanced, non-meat diet, but cats are carnivores (meat-eaters) and cannot. There are vegetarian dog foods on the market – ask in your local pet shop or veterinary surgery for details.

■ *What can you do?*

If you're thinking of getting a pet, ask yourself:

- Can you give it a good home?
- Can you give it the right amount of exercise and space?
- Can you afford to feed it properly?

- Can you ensure it will be looked after when you are away?
- Are you prepared to look after it for all its life?

If you do decide to go ahead, think about getting a pet from an animal rescue home. These animals are destroyed if homes are not found for them. Beware of pet shop animals and some breeders, as they may be selling dogs from puppy farms (see DOGS).

Lots of books on pet care are available from bookshops or public libraries. The RSPCA also publish information leaflets.

Consider having your pet NEUTEREd to avoid adding to the pet population. If you or your family are on a low income or receiving state benefit, you can apply for free veterinary treatment for your pet from the People's Dispensary for Sick Animals (PDSA).

Don't keep wild animals as pets. Houses and cages are not their natural habitat – see TRADE IN WILD ANIMALS.

Pigs

The popular image of a pig is a dirty, fat, unpleasant creature. When we want to degrade a person, we often call them a 'pig'. But pigs are not dirty or greedy animals – they are lively, clean, highly intelligent and very sociable. In fact, to be called a pig should be a great compliment!

Pigs have had a particularly rough deal down on the factory farm. About 8 million pigs are farmed in Britain to supply butchers and supermarkets with ham, bacon and pork. Most of these pigs are farmed indoors in cages, stalls and pens. Piglets are often taken from their mother at a very early age and reared in wire-mesh cages; they are then put in fattening pens, often with cold, concrete floors and no straw for bedding, and sometimes no light. The overcrowding, boredom and stress they suffer leads to tail-biting and other aggressive behaviour, so their tails are cut off (docked) to stop this happening.

For sows (female pigs), it gets worse. About 400,000 UK sows are kept in dry sow stalls, again with concrete floors and no bedding. The stalls are so small the sow cannot turn round; some are tethered to the floor to stop them moving. When a sow is ready to give birth (farrow) she is put into a farrowing crate – another tiny cage where she can only stand up or lie down. These crates were designed so that the piglets can suckle but prevent the sow from accidentally lying on them. A sow's natural behaviour is to build a nest when farrowing and to move around with her piglets.

Animal welfare groups have been campaigning for years to improve conditions for pigs against tough opposition from the farming lobby. In 1991, MPs received more letters on dry sow stalls than on the Gulf War! The government have now introduced regulations banning any new sow-stall systems and phasing out existing systems by 1999.

Other good news for pigs is the development of a new farrowing pen which allows sows to move without squashing their piglets, and the popularity of free-range meat, which means that more and more pigs now live outside in fields.

■ *What can you do?*

If you eat pig meat (ham, pork, bacon, lard, some sausages and pies), consider whether you want to carry on doing so or maybe go organic or free-range (see FOOD WITHOUT CRUELTY).

Support the work of Compassion in World Farming (CIWF), who can keep you up to date on all pig welfare issues through their magazine *Agscene*. They have a youth section called Farm Watch.

Tell people about the factory farming of pigs. CIWF sell bulk copies of leaflets on the pig industry which you can distribute to family, friends and neighbours, or put up on noticeboards.

See also FACTORY FARMING for other ideas for action.

Politics

British MPs from all parties say that the subject they receive most letters about is animal welfare. They are well aware that animal welfare measures are generally supported by the population at large – who, of course, are the voters.

There is a long history of concern for animals in Britain; animal welfare laws were first passed in 1822. Since then there have been many campaigns to influence the public, politicians and government. Some Bills have failed to get through Parliament; others have become law. Recent campaigns have focused on protecting badgers and the phasing out of veal crates. Today Britain is considered to have the best animal welfare record in Europe, but as Europe moves towards unity in 1992, it has become necessary to influence European Community (EC) laws and improve standards of animal welfare in all European countries.

Changes in the law and campaigns have up till now been piecemeal, relying on individual campaigns and individual MPs. There have been no overall animal welfare policies, but this is beginning to change. The three major political parties – the Conservative Party, the Labour Party and the Liberal Democrats – now have policies on animals as well as on the environment.

Another recent development has been the publication of the *Manifesto for Animals* by three of the main animal welfare organisations: the British Union for the Abolition of Vivisection, Compassion in World Farming, and Lynx. The *Manifesto* is a 'programme of political action for the 1990s'. It has been presented to all MPs and political parties and outlines a comprehensive policy for animal welfare with detailed sections on vivisection, farming and fur. Copies are available from any of the three organisations involved.

■ *What can you do?*

Find out exactly what the animal policies are of all the main political parties, or the one you support. Write to or ring them, asking what their position is on animal welfare issues in general or on any particular issue that interests you. You can also ask them to support the *Manifesto for Animals* (all MPs and political parties have received a copy).

You can write to your MP with the same questions, or with any issue you feel strongly about. Letters to MPs do count, so don't feel it's a waste of time. It is their job to represent your views in Parliament – they also want your vote!

Pollution

When you see a picture of an oil slick, it's easy to understand how pollution damages wildlife. In the Gulf War, after Iraqi troops deliberately released 11 million barrels of oil into the sea, millions of animals such as seabirds, sea mammals, insects and reptiles perished.

A lot of pollution is not so obvious. Waste and sewage are poured into the oceans all over the world; pesticides seep into the ground; factories pump out gases. All these pollutants and many more affect the ENVIRONMENT and the animals living in it, which includes us.

■ *What can you do?*

Pollution is a worldwide problem, but don't be overwhelmed by the scale of it. You *can* do something to help by reducing your impact on the planet. It's particularly important that people in Western countries change the way they live, because they consume the most. For example, a person in the developed world consumes on average 120 kg of paper and 450 kg of steel each year, whereas a person in a developing country consumes only 8 kg of paper and 43 kg of steel.

What you can do is use less, create less waste and reuse, repair and recycle whenever possible. Use 'environment-friendly' cleaning products and recycled paper. Tell other people what they can do too. The more people who change the way they live, the bigger the changes worldwide.

There are many ways to be less polluting and many excellent books to give you advice, such as *How to be Green* by John Button (Century Hutchinson, 1989) and *Blueprint for a Green Planet* by John Seymour and Herbert Girardet (Dorling Kindersley, 1987).

Leaflets and information are also available from Friends of the

Earth, the Tidy Britain Group, and many other environmental organisations.

Primates

Primates are a group of mammals which include monkeys, marmosets, baboons, chimpanzees, orang-utans, gorillas and humans. The genetic relationship between human and non-human primates is very close. Scientists have shown that proteins in chimpanzees are only 1 per cent different from those in humans. They are our closest relatives in the animal world.

It is this closeness which makes non-human primates suitable for experiments because they react in a biologically similar way to humans (see MEDICAL EXPERIMENTS, SPACE RESEARCH, VIVISECTION, WARFARE). In recent years many hundreds of primates have been used extensively in AIDS research. Ironically, it is their similarity to humans that makes their use in experiments all the more controversial, because they also feel pain and distress like us. We can identify easily with their suffering. Primates are highly intelligent, sociable animals, and the use of them in research laboratories has provoked outrage and anger in many people.

Some laboratories have breeding programmes to supply them with the primates they require, but it is estimated that in Britain 75 per cent are caught from the wild and exported. Many die during capture and transportation – for every chimpanzee reaching a laboratory alive, over five have died along the way. If they do survive they usually face a life of isolation, boredom and stress away from their natural family groups and habitat. They will also be subjected to various experiments, such as inhaling chemicals or having cancers induced in them. When the experiment is finished, they are killed and dissected. Many people see this trade in primates as a modern-day 'slave trade'.

Chimpanzees are also exploited for CIRCUSES and for 'snapshot' chimps worked by Spanish beach photographers (see HOLIDAYS). The Convention on International Trade in Endangered Species (CITES) has recently upgraded chimpanzees' status from 'threatened' to 'endangered', which should make exportation more difficult. However, with a live chimp worth $20,000 to a research laboratory, illegal trade is likely to continue. Other monkeys are not listed by CITES, and the trade continues.

■ *What can you do?*

Support campaigns run by Animal Aid, the Fund for the Replacement of Animals in Medical Experiments (FRAME), the International Primate Protection League, the RSPCA and Zoo Check. Write to your MP and the Home Secretary at the Home Office, calling for an end to the trade in wild primates and a ban on their use in experiments.

Protesting

It may be the raids on laboratories, bomb attacks and confrontation which get the most media coverage (see ANIMAL LIBERATION FRONT), but there are more effective ways of influencing people. Protest doesn't have to be violent or a confrontation. You can protest about something by not buying a certain product, by talking to your supermarket manager, by wearing a badge or T-shirt, or by sending a postcard!

The increase of cruelty-free cosmetics in shops is the result of constant pressure by thousands of ordinary people who wanted to live their beliefs and buy products not tested on animals. Changes in the law are often brought about by letter-writing campaigns, petitions and demonstrations. These are all ways of protesting; of expressing your point of view.

■ *What can you do?*

Write letters

Letter-writing is a very effective way of protesting. It brings your point of view to the attention of companies, organisations, local councils, government departments, MPs, Ministers, or whoever. If these people or organisations receive enough letters on a subject, they will realise that public opinion demands change.

When you're writing to protest:

- **Find out a name or job title to write to**, if possible. Your local library can help you find names and addresses of companies, MPs, etc.
- **Say why you're protesting** as clearly as you can. Back up your letter with further information such as an article or leaflet if you want to.
- **Say what you feel.** If you feel that something is cruel and barbaric say so, but be polite – you're much more likely to be taken seriously.
- **Ask for a reply** – say something like 'I look forward to hearing your opinion on this matter'.

Many animal rights organisations have letter-writing campaigns. In their magazines they will tell you whom they want people to write to, and why.

Petitions

If you feel strongly about something, you can organise a petition. If, for example, you want Wonder Cosmetics to stop testing their cosmetics on animals, you can write on a sheet of paper 'We, the undersigned, call on Wonder Cosmetics to stop testing cosmetic products on animals'. Draw columns for names, signatures and addresses. Then ask friends, family and anyone else you want if they will support you and sign the petition. Explain to them why you think they should. When you have collected as many signatures as you can, send the petition off.

Many animal welfare organisations frequently organise mass petitions to support their campaigns. Keep an eye on their magazines for details; you may also see petitions in health shops or natural beauty shops.

Demonstrations

Lots of animal rights organisations such as Animal Aid and Compassion in World Farming organise demonstrations, days of action, marches and leafleting campaigns, both locally and nationally. Contact them or look in their magazines for details.

See also JOINING GROUPS.

Psychological tests

Animals are routinely used in behaviour experiments in university and polytechnic psychology departments and research institutes. Some scientists believe that these studies of animal behaviour help the understanding of human behaviour, psychology and brain function, thereby benefiting people.

Animals are easier to study than people. Their behaviour is more obvious because they don't have layers of culture on top. They are also easier to control – for example, they can be kept in cages for long periods of time and there is no relationship between scientist and subject to complicate things. As with other types of experiments on animals, it would be considered immoral to use humans for many psychological tests.

Psychological tests have been used to research areas such as aggression, stress, isolation, overcrowding, starvation and maternal deprivation. There have been famous experiments to show what happens to a baby monkey if it is taken from its mother at birth; other tests have tried to induce mental illnesses or deliberately created brain damage in animals. Some have involved giving rats electric shocks to increase their aggression.

But does investigating behaviour such as aggression in rats imply that humans respond in the same way? Do scientists spend too much time and money looking at rats in the laboratory rather than at people in a city? Opponents of psychological tests on animals say that tests are unnecessary as well as cruel. One psychologist, Don Bannister, has said:

> Countless animals have been surgically dismembered, drugged, starved, fatigued, frozen, electrically shocked ...

maddened and killed in the belief that their behaviour, closely observed, would cast light on the nature of humankind.

■ *What can you do?*

Support campaigns against vivisection (see 'What can you do?' section under VIVISECTION).

If you're considering studying psychology at university or college, you may be expected to conduct experiments on animals (usually rats). When applying for courses, you can ask the department involved if this is part of the syllabus. If you're already studying in a psychology department and object to performing experiments, you can seek advice from the National Union of Students, the Student Campaign for Animal Rights, the Network of Individuals and Campaigns for Humane Education (NICHE), the British Union for the Abolition of Vivisection, the National Anti-Vivisection Society, or Animal Aid. You could also get together a petition calling for experiments to be banned – or at least optional – with like-minded students, and present it to the head of department.

See also DISSECTION.

Religious slaughter

British law says that animals for SLAUGHTER must be killed instantly or stunned so that they are 'insensible to pain' when they are killed, to prevent pain and suffering to animals at the abattoir. This does not apply to animals slaughtered according to strict Jewish or Muslim tradition. They have been exempted from the law in respect for their religious rules concerning killing animals for food. In both these traditions animals are not stunned before slaughter.

The traditional Jewish method of slaughter is called 'shechita'. It is carried out by specially trained and licensed Jewish slaughtermen, and only animals which are healthy and free of injury can be killed. They are despatched by a rapid cut deep into the neck. Jews do not eat the hindquarters of animals, so these cuts of meat usually go on to the open market.

The Muslim method is called 'halal', and Islamic law says that the name of God (Allah) must be spoken at the time of slaughter. Animals are also killed by cutting the throat. However, Islamic law also says that animals must be spared unnecessary pain, and because of this many Muslims will eat pre-stunned animals.

The debate over whether Jews and Muslims should conform to British law has raged for many years. Animal welfare groups say that religious slaughter causes terror and pain in animals, and they do not die instantly. The Farm Animal Welfare Council and the British Veterinary Association wish to see a ban on religious methods of slaughter, and call for the stunning of all animals before they are killed. Successive governments have refused to change the law so as not to offend these religious groups.

Religious slaughter is a difficult issue because it touches on religious freedoms and the rights of minority ethnic groups. If a country gives religious groups the freedom to have their own rituals and traditions, what happens when those traditions are against the law of that country? How far should religious freedom go? Religious traditions would not be allowed if they harmed people or property. Should religious groups be allowed different rules when it comes to animals?

Unfortunately, the debate can often be confused with racial or religious prejudice rather than concern for animal welfare.

■ *What can you do?*

Consider your views on religious slaughter – do you think religious freedom is more important than animal welfare? Find out more from the Humane Slaughter Association, the RSPCA or Compassion in World Farming. All produce leaflets explaining the subject in more detail.

If you are Jewish or Muslim and do not wish to eat meat slaughtered by traditional methods, you could consider becoming a VEGETARIAN.

Animal groups are calling for meat from religious slaughter to be labelled so that it can be identified if it reaches non-Jewish or non-Muslim shops. So far, the government have ignored these calls. You can write to your MP asking for his or her views on the subject.

Reptiles

Reptiles are one of the most mistreated animal groups, and the scale of abuse is enormous. Because reptiles are cold-blooded, we assume that they can't feel pain like us. In fact, cold-blooded animals may suffer more than warm-blooded ones because they have a very slow metabolic rate and therefore take longer to die.

Crocodilians (crocodiles, caiman and alligators) are both caught in the wild and ranched. They are trapped and hunted by a variety of gruesome methods and are frequently skinned alive. They may also be decapitated alive so the heads can be used as curios and ornaments – the heads can take over one hour to die. The skins are used only for luxury goods such as crocodile shoes, handbags and belts.

Turtles are harpooned, hooked, netted or captured while returning to their traditional breeding sites. They may not be killed instantly but taken to markets and restaurants, where their flesh is carved off in pieces while they are still alive. This prevents the meat rotting in the tropical climate. They die when so much is carved off that they cannot live any longer.

Snakes are particularly loathed and feared by humans, and they suffer accordingly. Despite the fact that only 10 per cent of all snakes are poisonous to humans, most species are ruthlessly killed when they come into contact with us. The American rattlesnake is just one example of a species in decline, with over 300,000 rounded up and killed each year. Rattlesnake round-ups, as they are called, are accompanied by shows of horrendous cruelty to the snakes, many designed to show how brave and 'macho' the handlers are. Snakes may be thrown, kicked, gouged, and set alight alive.

The list of abuses against reptiles goes on and on. Most species have been on the earth at least as long as humans, and some millions of years longer. It seems high time for a change in human attitudes towards these ancient and beautiful creatures.

■ *What can you do?*

The Trust for the Protection of Reptiles can help you with leaflets and information. They also run campaigns you can support.

Don't buy wild-animal products such as skins, lizard-head key rings, belts and stuffed animals, either here or when abroad. It is illegal to import many of them into Britain anyway – see TRADE IN WILD ANIMALS.

Road accidents

Often the only time we see wildlife is when it's crossing the road or grazing by the roadside, but each year millions of animals are killed on the roads – many more than are killed by hunting and shooting. In Britain, the victims are usually hedgehogs, rabbits, foxes, badgers and birds. It is estimated that 47,500 badgers and 3,000–5,000 barn owls are killed every year. They are usually run over in the early morning or evening – often in spring, when they are out and about feeding. Often their pathways and routes cross roads. The animals may be killed instantly, or they may crawl away injured. Some die in their burrows; others recover.

Domestic animals are also often road accident victims. Stray or uncontrolled dogs and cats do sometimes run out on to the road, into the path of a passing car. An accident involving a dog must be reported to the police.

Killing an animal on the road can be very distressing, especially as there's often very little you can do if it runs out in front of your car.

■ *What can you do?*

If you drive, be alert for animals on the roadside that may want to cross. Don't speed – especially around country lanes at night, when you might not be able to stop in time.

If you find an injured animal by the roadside, be careful. Approach it calmly, but do not touch it. Some wild animals, such as foxes and badgers, can give you a nasty bite. Instead, telephone the local RSPCA inspector, a local vet, wildlife hospital, animal rescue centre, nature conservation group or badger group, telling them:

- the type of animal involved;
- what you think the injuries might be;
- whether the animal is loose or restrained;
- the precise location of the animal.

If you think the animal will crawl away before help arrives, place a large cardboard or wooden box (with airholes in) over it and put a weight on top (or sit on it). Darkness is often calming for a frightened animal.

The RSPCA publish the leaflets *First Aid for Animals* (which has a section on road accidents) and *Care of Sick, Injured and Orphaned Birds*.

The National Federation of Badger Groups can help with locating your local group, and the British Hedgehog Preservation Society can help with information on injured hedgehogs.

School animals

You can learn a lot from watching and looking after animals, and keeping them in school can be fun, but it may not be such fun for the animals themselves unless they are well looked after. The animals most commonly kept in schools are gerbils, mice, rats, guinea pigs and hamsters, but sometimes schools have mini-farms with chickens and rabbits. Stick insects are another favourite, and frogspawn and tadpoles often put in a seasonal appearance.

There are a few points to think about before getting an animal for the classroom (or if you've already got one):

- Is keeping the animal in school threatening its survival?
- Consider the alternatives – could you learn more from videos, books or discussions?
- Can you cater for the animal's needs such as food, exercise, housing, security, space, companionship? Do you know enough about the animal's biology to do this?
- Can you provide care during the week, weekends and holidays?
- Is veterinary treatment available if necessary?
- Are the humans in school (this includes teachers!) safe?
- Does someone have overall responsibility for looking after the animals?

Wild animals are not suitable as school pets, and any animals brought in from the wild for study (such as pond creatures) must be returned to their habitat after the lesson. They are not disposable study aids; they are living animals.

■ *What can you do?*

If your class is thinking about getting an animal, you can ask your teacher if you can discuss it first and look at the points outlined here. If you've already got animals in school, have these points been considered?

If you're not happy with the preparations for an animal coming into school or the conditions for animals already there, you could:

- take the matter to school council, if there is one;
- form a group of friends who feel the same way and speak to a teacher, headteacher, parents' association or school governors;
- in extreme cases, contact the RSPCA.

The RSPCA publish two booklets which outline the welfare and legal aspects of keeping animals in schools: *Animals in Schools* and *Small Mammals in Schools*; the RSPCA Education Department can also help with advice.

Shooting

Shooting is one of the most popular activities in Europe. It can be for sport or for PEST CONTROL; it can be legal or illegal (poaching). Many different animals are shot. In wildfowling, ducks and geese are killed; in game-shooting it is pheasants, partridge, grouse, elk or deer (deer-stalking); and in pest-control measures it is usually rabbits, squirrels, pigeons and deer. Some birds, such as pheasant and partridge, are reared especially for shooting. In Southern Europe there is mass shooting of MIGRATING BIRDS, as well as the hunting of wild boar and brown bear.

Each year in Britain about 600,000 people shoot regularly, killing 10 million pheasants, 12 million pigeons, 1 million ducks, 500,000 grouse, 150,000 woodcock and 300,000 hares. There are controls on 'closed seasons' when animals cannot be shot, and strict gun laws.

The pro-shooting lobby say that it is vital to control animal populations (culling) which would otherwise become a pest to farmers and foresters. They also say that shooting is a popular and traditional country sport, and they have as much right to shoot a grouse as a fox does to kill a rabbit. They also often say that hunters respect nature and intelligent, thoughtful hunting is a valid and useful sport.

The anti-shooting lobby say that although many animals are killed instantly by the bullet, many are not and may suffer a prolonged and painful death. They also say that to maintain stocks of grouse and pheasant for the gun, their natural predators, such as foxes and birds of prey, are ruthlessly killed by game-keepers. (It is estimated that gamekeepers kill 4 million animals a year.) Keeping high populations of game birds may also upset the natural ecological balance of an area.

How you feel about shooting may depend on whether you think animals have a right to a free life unharmed by humans. Some animal rights groups oppose shooting purely because of this belief; others oppose shooting as unnecessary and cruel.

Culling wild animals also raises questions. Should humans control wild-animal populations? If they don't, what will happen? In Scotland, it is argued that if the red deer were not culled their numbers would increase dramatically, causing ecological damage to farmland and other wildlife habitats.

■ *What can you do?*

Think about the issues involved. Find out more from the League Against Cruel Sports, the British Association for Shooting and Conservation, the British Field Sports Society.

Slaughter

The slaughter of animals is a subject few people will think about, let alone discuss. They would rather not know how animals become cuts of meat for their dinner-table. Their blinkered view is aided by the food industry, which produces meat in tidy, wrapped packages giving few clues to their animal origin. Yet slaughter is a huge industry, and essential if we continue to need the efficient killing of animals for food.

In Britain in 1988 over 3 million cattle, 15 million pigs, 17 million sheep and a staggering 450 million poultry birds were killed for meat in 940 slaughterhouses or abattoirs. In most Western countries the procedure and regulations concerning slaughter are similar. Animals must be stunned before killing, and this is carried out by a fired bolt or electrical stunner. These methods are effective if used properly, but sometimes they are carelessly used and animals are still conscious when they are killed. After stunning, the animals are hung up by one leg and the throat is cut to drain the blood out. Blood loss should be quick to cause brain failure and death, but again there are many reports of careless and inaccurate handling.

Next, the meat is tenderised by electrically stimulating the flesh before the carcass is butchered. Animal welfare organisations want this practice banned. They say that in the speed of the slaughterhouse operations other procedures may not be carried out properly and the electric shock may cause animals to recover some consciousness. Meat can also be tenderised by an injection of drugs just before slaughter, but Compassion in World Farming believe this causes distress in animals and 'is the final insult to already stressed creatures'.

There are many animal welfare issues surrounding slaughter – the sale of animals at MARKETS and their TRANSPORT to abattoirs. Many arrive in an already stressed and fearful condition. They may be beaten or goaded with electric goads to make them move around at the abattoir. There are regulations concerning animal welfare at abattoirs, and some have an official vet in attendance. Responsibility for abattoirs lies with the local authority. It is up to them to enforce welfare laws, but there are many cases of widespread cruelty to animals by staff.

The speed and scale of the operation reduces the whole operation to that of a conveyor-belt factory – live animals go in one end and cuts of meat come out the other. One aspect to consider is: how do we want our food animals to live and to die? Do they have a right to some dignity in their death? Should they be killed on the farm rather than in abattoirs? Research is under way to design a mobile slaughterhouse so that animals can be killed on the farm rather than transported to abattoirs.

The Russian writer of *War and Peace*, Leo Tolstoy, said, 'As long as there are slaughterhouses there will be battlefields.'

■ *What can you do?*

In 1984 the Farm Animal Welfare Council surveyed slaughter-houses in Britain and put forward over a hundred recommendations for change. To date only eighteen have been adopted by the Ministry of Agriculture. You can write to your MP expressing your feelings about slaughterhouse practice and asking for the recommendations to be implemented.

Find out more from Compassion in World Farming and the Humane Slaughter Association. Support their campaigns.

Consider your diet – see VEGETARIANS. See also PETS, RELIGIOUS SLAUGHTER.

Space research

'That's one small step for man, one giant leap for mankind' are the words astronaut Neil Armstrong spoke when he became the first human to walk on the moon. It was not, however, such a good step for many animals.

In all countries with space programmes, but especially in the USA and former Soviet Union, animals have been used in space experiments and space flights. Rats, dogs, chimpanzees, insects, frogs and fish have all been launched into orbit. The first living being ever to go into space was a dog named Laika. Laika was fired into orbit by the Soviet space programme in 1957 and survived for one week before dying in orbit. In the USA monkeys have undergone 'astronaut training', gone into space (with electrodes implanted in their brain) and been killed and dissected on their return to earth.

One or two space animals have survived, only to be used for

propaganda purposes. This is a description, from a film on the American space programme, of a 'space-chimp' now on show in a zoo:

> New heroes are born every day but the nation still honours a bold pioneer who led the way in the best traditions of the great American frontiersmen. Today he basks in the glow of his memories among the peaceful surroundings of the National Zoological Park in Washington: astronaut Ham, the space chimpanzee.

This glowing description portrays an image of the hero-monkey, but this chimpanzee and other animal astronauts must have experienced distress and terror, usually followed by death. Animals are still being used in space research.

■ *What can you do?*

If you disagree with sending animals into space, write to:

- National Aeronautics and Space Administration, 400 Maryland Avenue, Washington DC SW 20546, USA;
- the Ambassador, United States Embassy, 24 Grosvenor Square, London W1A 1AE;
- the Ambassador, United Soviet Socialist Republics Embassy, 13 Kensington Palace Gardens, London W8 4QX;
- the Director, European Space Agency, 8–10 rue Mario Nikis, F-75738 Paris Cedex 15, France;

calling for an end to the use of animals in space research.

If you see examples in newspapers and magazines of animals being portrayed as space heroes, you can write to the editor and complain.

Speciesism

This is a term used by some animal rights campaigners to describe human treatment of other animals. Humans treat other animals differently from the way they treat other humans, and animal rights activists see this as discrimination. Discrimination means singling out a group for favour or disfavour, and in our society it's most often used in relation to race, gender, sexuality or disability. In this case it is discrimination against animals because they are not human.

For example, 'speciesists' would ask: why do we use a highly intelligent chimpanzee in MEDICAL EXPERIMENTS yet would never think of using a retarded human being who may have a lower mental level? Their answer: the only reason is that a chimpanzee is not human. This is speciesism.

Martyn Ford, in *Towards Animal Rights*, says, 'Animals have been denied moral rights because, quite simply, they do not belong to our own species.'

■ *What can you do?*

Think about speciesism, and whether you agree with it or not. Are humans and animals equal, or do you think humans are a superior species?

See also ANIMAL RIGHTS, DIFFERENT CULTURES, DIFFERENT OPINIONS, and KINSHIP.

Trade in wild animals

Animals are big business. Around the world they are bought and sold in their millions. Much of this trade – such as horse sales – is legal, but some, such as trade in ENDANGERED SPECIES, is illegal. Animals are traded for food, sport, furs, pets; for research laboratories and zoos.

One of the biggest areas of concern is the trade in wild birds. Over 8 million wild birds, such as parrots and macaws, are caught in the wild each year in countries such as Senegal, India, China, Indonesia, Tanzania and Argentina. They are exported to Europe to be kept as pets. A recent report by the Environmental Investigation Agency (EIA) has revealed the size of the trade and the extent of the cruelty inflicted on these birds. Many die in traps set for them, or crammed in cages by the bird collector. The survivors are bought by an exporter, packed into crates and airfreighted abroad. Many more die during transport or in quarantine in their host country. For every bird reaching the pet shop, three have died on the way. The survivors, once wild in their forest habitat, are then condemned to spend the rest of their life in a cage. The scale of the operation decimates the populations of these birds in the wild. Forty-one species (thirty parrot species) are directly threatened by this trade. The story is the same with other wild species such as TROPICAL FISH, PRIMATES and terrapins.

New York State has banned the import of wild birds and some airlines, such as Virgin, Lufthansa and Swissair, now refuse to carry live birds. There is a Campaign to Ban the Import of Wild

Birds to Europe, because the European Community is the world's largest importer of wild birds.

■ *What can you do?*

Don't keep – or encourage others to keep – a wild animal as a pet. If you're not sure which animals are wild species, ask the RSPCA Wildlife Department for advice. If you want a pet, there are plenty of domesticated animals which want good homes in rescue centres.

If you see a pet shop or market stall selling wild animals, ask them who and where the animal breeder is. If you don't get a satisfactory answer, you can write to them explaining about the cruelties of the trade and asking them to stop. If you still get no response or are concerned about the welfare of animals, contact the RSPCA Wildlife Department or the Environmental Investigation Agency (EIA) for advice.

The RSPCA and EIA 'Ban the Wild Bird Trade' Campaign is asking people to write to their MEP (Member of the European Parliament) urging him or her to support a ban. You can find out who your MEP is from your local library, or by contacting the European Parliament Information Office. More information on how you can support the campaign is available from the RSPCA.

The Trust for the Protection of Reptiles campaign against the trade in reptiles. See also ENDANGERED SPECIES, FROGS' LEGS.

Transport of live animals

Imagine what it's like to be stuck on a packed bus for twenty-four hours with no food, water or toilet. It's not a situation anyone would want, yet thousands of animals endure terrifying journeys packed into lorries. Sometimes their journey is short – to the local abattoir – but at other times they are being exported abroad for SLAUGHTER.

Animals are loaded into multi-deck lorries with no food or water and driven hundreds of miles to countries such as Spain to be slaughtered for the Spanish market. They may be handled badly at either end of their journey – they are unlikely to be given any periods of rest. Currently European law requires animals to be offered food and water after twenty-four hours unless the journey can be completed within a 'reasonable time thereafter'. It is difficult to imagine the terror, suffering and stress felt by the animals.

As trade within the European Community (EC) has increased, so has the number of animals being exported, and with the prospect of reduced trade restrictions in 1992 the numbers could grow even more. Apart from the cruelty of transporting animals over such distances, there is also concern that abattoirs in other European countries are well below UK standards. At present, horses and ponies cannot be exported for slaughter, but new EC regulations in 1992 could change this, allowing horses to be exported for the continental horsemeat market.

Animal welfare groups have been campaigning hard to end the suffering of animals transported around Europe. An RSPCA petition signed by two million people was presented to the EC Council of Agricultural Ministers in 1991. It demands new European legislation to ensure that:

- all food animals are slaughtered as near as possible to the farm where they are raised;
- journeys to abattoirs are limited to eight hours;
- laws to prevent the export of live horses and ponies are kept in place;
- a certification scheme is set up to make sure animals are properly treated while travelling and receive adequate rest, food and water.

■ *What can you do?*

Support the campaigns run by the RSPCA and Compassion in World Farming. They can also send you further information on this issue.

Write to your MP, MEP (Member of the European Parliament), Minister of Agriculture and the President of the Council of Agricultural Ministers at the European Commission, calling for an end to this unnecessary suffering.

If you see on lorries animals that you think are being ill-treated or left at docks or ports for an unreasonable amount of time, contact the local RSPCA inspector (look in the telephone book under 'Royal Society').

Trapping

Trapping is used worldwide to catch animals for food, FUR, and because they are considered a PEST. There are various methods of trapping.

Snares: Snares are loops of wire which are set in the ground and pull tight around an animal's leg when it steps in, trapping the animal. They are used by gamekeepers to control animals preying on game birds; in Northern countries by fur-trappers; and in Southern Europe to catch songbirds. In the UK it is not a criminal offence to set a snare for a wild animal, but the Wildlife and Countryside Act 1981 calls for snares to be inspected every twenty-four hours. However, this law is largely unenforceable.

Leghold traps (gin trap): This brutal trap works by catching the animal's leg in the steel jaws of the trap. Animals are not killed instantly and, in their desperation to escape, may gnaw or wring their own leg off. They may be trapped in agony for several days before the hunter returns to finish them off by clubbing, suffocation or strangulation.

The leghold trap has been banned by 64 countries including Britain, where it was outlawed in 1958 as a 'diabolical instrument which causes an incredible amount of suffering'. It is thought, however, that some traps are still being used illegally. In Canada and the USA the traps are not illegal, but some States require that they are inspected at regular intervals. The European Community has drawn up draft laws to ban the trap in Europe and ban fur imports from the USA, Canada and the former Soviet Union if they continue to use leghold traps.

Limed twigs: In Southern Europe millions of MIGRATING BIRDS are trapped each year. In Spain, for example, 30 million small birds, such as warblers and robins, are trapped in nets baited with ants or by smearing twigs with sticky lime. The perching birds become stuck on the twigs and are later collected and usually eaten by the hunter.

Nets: Nets may also be used to catch birds, again in Southern Europe. A decoy bird is placed in a cage nearby and its singing attracts other birds which become entangled in the net.

In nearly all types of traps, animals struggle to free themselves, inflicting appalling injuries and suffering. Traps are also indiscriminate – they kill anything, not just the species they are intended to catch.

■ *What can you do?*

See the 'What can you do?' sections on FUR, MIGRATING BIRDS, PEST CONTROL.

Tribal peoples

There are over 200 million tribal people in the world today. They are groups such as the Aborigines in Australia or the Bushmen in southern Africa living traditional lives. They are often thought of as 'primitive' or 'Stone-age' because they don't lead 'advanced or civilised' lives like us in Western-style societies. Many tribes have been persecuted, colonised or treated as a tourist attraction in the name of progress.

Tribes are usually self-supporting and live by hunting, fishing, herding or farming, and they have their own customs and traditions. Far from being primitive, they often live in closer harmony with their ENVIRONMENT than we do. They are no better or worse than us – they are just different.

The tribes' traditional way of life has come into conflict with animal welfare campaigners. In the Canadian Arctic, the Inuit people hunt seals for their FUR and meat. Traditionally, they have taken only what they need, but as demand from North America and Europe for the soft, white fur of harp seal pups increased, they developed their industry to supply these markets. The seals were clubbed to death and skinned on the Arctic ice. In the late 1980s several groups campaigned hard to stop the killing. They succeeded, and the European Community and American government banned imports of seal products. The Inuit economy collapsed, and many were left without jobs or money.

One exemption from the world ban on WHALING is tribal 'subsistence whaling'. To Alaskan Inuit people, whaling is part of their traditional life. They catch about 35 bowhead whales a year from small walrus-skin boats. Many people feel that this whaling should be banned too, but others support the Inuit's right to hunt whales as they have always done. Like many tribal peoples, the Inuit have a close – even spiritual – relationship with other animals and the environment. They have great respect for the animals they kill.

Cases like these show how complicated the issues are. Is a traditional culture which has lived in harmony with its animals and environment for centuries more important than animal welfare? Are we in Western societies trying to impose our ideas and morals on other societies? In southern Africa, the Bushmen have been evicted from their traditional lands to make a nature reserve – what are their rights? Are wild and endangered animals more important than tribal peoples?

■ *What can you do?*

Think about the animal issues involved. As with many other animal issues, you may not be able to decide where you stand. It's OK to be uncertain, but you may find it helpful to get more facts.

The plight of tribal peoples has been recognised by many organisations and governments, although others seek to evict them from their land. Survival International is a group which works for the rights of threatened tribal peoples. They can provide you with further information, and run campaigns you can support. Organise a discussion group, talk or film show on tribal peoples. Survival International have a selection of films, videos and slidesets for hire.

Tropical fish

Tanks of tropical fish are popular in dentists' waiting-rooms and people's living-rooms, especially in Europe and North America, where there are about two million households with aquaria. There is a large and profitable international trade in tropical marine and freshwater fish. Over two million live freshwater fish were imported to Britain in 1988 – of these, 90 per cent were commercially bred in the Far East; the rest were collected from the wild.

The import and export of tropical fish species is causing many wild populations of fish to become badly depleted. In particular the delicate and colourful coral reef fish are threatened (the increase in tourism in these areas is also a threat – see HOLIDAYS). Like so many other wild animals which are bought and sold, many of these fish die while being captured or in transit. About 80 per cent of wild-caught fish die before even reaching the exporter. Fish imported to Britain must have a Ministry of Agriculture, Fisheries and Food licence, but many are imported illegally.

Once in the aquarium or glass bowl, tropical fish are not often in an ideal environment. We may think they are because they're in water, but in their natural state they would have much more than this. Many fish species forage and roam large distances on coral reefs. Once captive in the tank they are deprived of the space and activity they need, and often the company of others of their own species. Like many other captive animals (see ZOOS) their movement is confined to swimming up and down the tank. Unless they are well kept they may suffer from the wrong water temperature or fluctuating water temperature, as well as chemicals such as fly spray or smoke being absorbed into the water. Fish in aquaria die much younger than those in the wild. Tropical fish are wild animals – the open seas and oceans are their natural habitat.

■ *What can you do?*

If you keep – or want to keep – tropical fish, buy them only from a reputable dealer who buys commercially bred fish. Make sure you know how to look after them properly. There are lots of books on the subject in public libraries, and reputable aquarists' shops can help you too. The Federation of British Aquatic Societies can also help with further information.

Veal

The light-coloured meat from young calves is highly prized by some chefs and gourmets, but the story of veal production is much less appetising. The calves are taken from their mothers a few days after birth and put into 'veal crates'. Once in the crates they remain there until they are slaughtered, at about fourteen weeks old. They cannot turn round or move forwards or backwards, as exercise ruins the texture of the veal meat. They often have no straw for bedding or contact with other animals, and may be kept in darkness. To keep the meat light-coloured they are fed only on milky liquids low in iron, and have no fibre in their diet. This makes them anaemic and 'white-fleshed'.

Veal crates have now been banned in Britain because of the extreme cruelty they inflict on the calves, but this has had little effect on the veal market. Now calves are transported live to other European countries where crates are not banned. In 1990, over 300,000 calves were exported to crates in France and Holland. These calves may face long journeys in appalling conditions (see TRANSPORT OF LIVE ANIMALS). After slaughter the veal is imported back to butchers and restaurants in Britain.

Some free-range veal is now being produced, but most veal comes from the millions of crates on farms in other European countries.

■ *What can you do?*

If you eat meat, don't eat veal unless you're sure it's free-range. If you see veal in supermarkets or restaurants, you can write to the manager or owner telling him or her about the veal trade and asking them to stop selling it.

Write to your MP asking him or her to support a ban on veal imports to Britain, and to your MEP (Member of the European Parliament) calling for a ban on veal crates within the European Community.

Vegans

Vegans have chosen not to eat or use animal products at all. This means they eat no flesh, fish, fowl, milk, honey, dairy products or eggs or products containing them such as some cakes, pies and pastries, or gelatine-based products such as jelly. Strict vegans also seek, as far as possible, to use no animal products in their life. This includes leather clothing and shoes, silk, wool, duck-down and many other animal products.

What vegans do eat is grains, pulses, seeds, nuts, fruit and vegetables. They say that all the nutrients we need can be provided in a balanced and varied vegan diet, and they get enough protein from pulses, beans, soya products, grains and nuts.

Becoming a vegan involves taking more responsibility for your food and nutritional requirements and planning for yourself a good diet. This is a good idea anyway. A vegan diet does contain a lot of vitamins and minerals because vegans usually eat plenty of fresh food and are also more knowledgeable about their food.

■ What can you do?

Think about your diet and what animal products you use in your life. If you want to and can change, you might find it easier to cut animal products out of your life gradually.

Have a look at vegan cookbooks in the library or bookshop (see book list on page 156) and find out what sorts of food you need for a good diet.

You can get further information from the Vegan Society.

Vegetarians

There is a lot of debate over whether meat is necessary to the human diet, but humans have probably been eating animals since 2 million years BC. Humans are usually considered to be omnivores, which means we can eat most types of food.

What is a vegetarian? Someone who does not eat fish, flesh or fowl. Vegetarians eat vegetables, fruit, grains such as wheat and rice, pulses such as lentils, beans, nuts and seeds. Some eat dairy products and eggs because these do not involve the SLAUGHTER of animals. A well-balanced vegetarian diet includes all the nutrients humans need.

Vegetarians often face a lot of criticism from meat-eaters. They are also sometimes called faddy eaters or cranks but, if they are cranks, there are more and more of them every day. There are about 3.6 million vegetarians in Britain, and 28,000 people give up meat each week. In the USA there are about 9 million vegetarians. Many more people have reduced their intake of meat and fish.

Many people are changing their diet for health reasons. Research has shown that vegetarians have 75 per cent less cancer-causing substances (carcinogens) in their bodies than meat-eaters, and their cancer rate is 30 per cent lower. The higher amount of fibre in the diet gives better action in the gut and less constipation! One study showed that vegetarians spend less time in hospital.

Another reason many people give up meat is that they don't want to contribute to the animal suffering involved in FACTORY FARMING and slaughter. Others give ecological reasons. Large-scale livestock farming can pollute the environment; animal sewage (slurry) is over a hundred times more polluting than human sewage. Livestock farming is also not very efficient. Ten hectares of land will support 61 people on a vegetarian diet of soya beans; 24 on a diet of wheat and 2 on a diet of beef. More vegetarians could mean less famine.

Some people feel that it is morally wrong to eat animals, and many great thinkers and spiritual leaders – such as Gandhi, Tolstoy and Leonardo da Vinci – have been vegetarians. Another famous vegetarian, the playwright George Bernard Shaw, said, 'Animals are my friends . . . and I don't eat my friends.'

So why does anyone eat meat? Well, they like the taste and texture and it's what they've always done! Meat-eaters say that meat protein is needed for growth and strength and we are designed to eat meat. You may often hear meat-eaters say that animals are on the earth for our use, and what would happen to farm animals if we didn't eat them?

■ *What can you do?*

Think about your diet. If you eat meat now, do you want to give it up or reduce the amount you eat? It's cheaper and healthier to be vegetarian but it may be difficult to change, especially if you're not in control of the cooking. You may also face some opposition from meat-eating family and friends. However, have the courage of your convictions and know that thousands of people a week are joining you.

If you don't think you can change overnight, you can start by giving up meat on one day a week or for one meal a day. Eat cheese rather than ham sandwiches or, if you're having a take-away, veggieburger or pizza rather than hamburger.

There are lots of vegetarian cookbooks in libraries and book-shops. Look at them for information on what to eat for a healthy diet, and for recipes.

If you are at school, college or work you can ask the canteen to provide vegetarian meals, and if you study home economics ask for vegetarian recipes to be included. The Vegetarian Society can help with recipes and dietary advice.

If you're eating out, ask for a vegetarian meal if you don't see one on the menu. The more people ask, the more restaurants will change.

If you are a vegetarian, cook a meatless meal for your friends so that they can taste for themselves how good vegetarian food can be.

More information is available from the Vegetarian Society and Animal Aid. If you want information from the meat industry, contact the Meat and Livestock Commission.

Vivisection

Although 'vivisection' literally means cutting open live animals to carry out experiments, it is now a general term for the use of animals in experiments. Live animals are used in experiments to see the effects on living bodies of drugs and medicines, COSMETICS AND TOILETRIES, household cleaners, food additives and other chemicals. They are also used in experimental medical surgery to test new operations, PSYCHOLOGICAL TESTS, WARFARE and SPACE RESEARCH.

The most commonly used animals are rats and mice, with rabbits, guinea pigs, hamsters, gerbils, cats, dogs, horses, pigs, sheep, cattle, birds, fish, amphibians and PRIMATES also used in large numbers. Most animals are bred in captivity, but some are caught in the wild. It is considered morally unacceptable to experiment on humans, so other animals are used because of the similarity in their biology and body processes. Also, they are easy to control and can be killed and dissected. Each year 200 million animals worldwide are killed in experiments.

In most countries, anyone involved in research has to abide by laws which ensure that animals are housed properly and treated carefully to reduce unnecessary pain and distress. In Britain experiments are covered by the Animals (Scientific Procedures) Act 1986. Most research is carried out in commercial laboratories, universities, polytechnics and medical schools.

Many experiments are carried out to test the safety of a product. The main tests used are:

The **LD50 (Lethal Dose 50 per cent Test)**, in which animals, usually rats and mice, are force-fed a substance until 50 per cent of them die. The time taken for death to occur shows how poisonous the substance is.

The **Draize Eye Test**, which is used to test for irritation to the eye. Cosmetics such as shampoo or hairspray are dripped into the eye of an animal, usually a rabbit, for up to seven days. Rabbits are used because they do not produce tears, which would wash the substance away. The degree of redness, swelling, ulceration and discharge on the eye is measured.

Skin irritancy tests, which involve shaving the skin of an animal, usually guinea pigs and rabbits, and applying the substance. The skin reaction is then observed.

Laboratories in Britain used 3,315,125 animals in 1989 for the following types of experiments:

drugs, medical, dental, veterinary	1,158,561
pesticides and herbicides	80,692
industrial chemicals	86,252
household products	4,017
food additives	5,710
cosmetics	12,090
tobacco	387
alcohol research	1,114
education	12,099

73,531 animals were deliberately given cancer, and over two-thirds of all experiments were carried out without anaesthetic (however, some experiments, such as blood tests, may not need an anaesthetic).

■ *What can you do?*

Find out more. Animal Aid, the British Union for the Abolition of Vivisection, the National Anti-Vivisection Society and the RSPCA all oppose animal experiments and publish many leaflets and reports.

Consider the other point of view. The Research Defence Society and Animals in Medicines Research Information Centre (AMRIC) support the use of animals in experiments. They can also send you information.

See ALTERNATIVES TO ANIMAL EXPERIMENTS, HOMES AND GARDENS, and MEDICAL EXPERIMENTS for action ideas.

Warfare

Millions of humans have died in wars, but there is also a largely untold story of animals and war. Millions of animals have also died for war and defence. Some, such as the cavalry horses in the First World War, died on the battlefield; others, such as DOL-PHINS, have been trained to guard military installations and plant mines. In the Falklands War, whales were mistakenly torpedoed because they looked like Argentinian submarines on the radar. Countless other animals have died in the name of defence research.

Secrecy surrounds the defence world, making it difficult to know how many animals are being used in research. It has been estimated that at least 9,200 (including dogs, pigs, sheep, rats and PRIMATES) were used in the UK in 1987. Warfare research includes nuclear weapons testing, in which animals are exposed to deadly doses of radiation to assess the effects and death rates, and biological warfare testing, in which animals are infected with deadly diseases.

In chemical warfare experiments animals are gassed with nerve and riot-control gas; injected, skin- and eye-tested with deadly chemicals, often without anaesthetic. These chemicals are designed to kill people and must inflict extreme pain and suffering on test animals. In the late 1980s the world was outraged when Iraq used chemicals against the Kurdish people, and there is widespread condemnation of their use. However, chemicals continue to be researched and tested on animals in many countries.

In Britain the work is mostly done at the Chemical Defence Establishment at Porton Down in Wiltshire.

Another area of warfare experiments is weapons testing, where animals are wounded or killed to test the efficiency of guns or ammunition. There are documented cases of dogs and goats being shot in the legs, pigs used to practise battlefield surgery and monkeys used in aircraft crash simulations to test ejector seats. In all these cases – from different countries around the world – the animals die, but only after painful and sometimes prolonged suffering.

■ What can you do?

The defence industry is highly secretive and very powerful. It is difficult to find out information on which to base complaints. Although in the USA the Freedom of Information Act allows people to find out more about animal experiments, in Britain there is no such law. However, you can write to your MP asking them for their views on warfare experiments involving animals and pressing for freedom of information in Britain.

Find out more. A booklet, *The Military Abuse of Animals*, published by the British Union for the Abolition of Vivisection (BUAV), gives good background information to the subject.

Support campaigns by Animal Aid, BUAV and the National Anti-Vivisection Society. The Campaign for Nuclear Disarmament (CND) can provide you with more information on nuclear and chemical warfare.

See also SPACE RESEARCH.

Whaling

Humans are newcomers on the earth compared to whales. These great creatures of the deep have been living on earth much longer than us. They have larger brains than humans and are capable of sophisticated mental processes. They may be more intelligent than humans. They have a whale 'language' – complex song cycles they communicate to each other across huge stretches of ocean. They are also at least as social as humans. Whales, superb swimmers and divers, are perfectly adapted to their ocean environment.

Whales have fascinated and attracted humans for centuries, but the treatment of whales by humans is one of the more shameful episodes in human history. We have killed them relentlessly for their meat, blubber (fat) and whale oil. As we developed faster ships and deadlier technology, the scale of the killing increased, so that species after species of whale were hunted almost to extinction.

As whale numbers decreased, environmental groups launched a huge and successful campaign to 'save the whale'. Many countries stopped whaling, but some nations refused to stop. Whaling is regulated by the International Whaling Commission (IWC), which is responsible for quota systems to limit the number of whales killed. In 1986 they imposed the first-ever ban on whaling. There were exceptions to this ban, such as whales hunted by traditional methods by TRIBAL PEOPLES and whales caught for scientific research. In 1991 the ban was renewed for a year, but Iceland, Norway and Japan want to reintroduce quotas for commercial whaling. The Japanese have a great taste for whale meat and there is evidence that whales caught for 'scientific purposes' end up on restaurant tables in Japan, where whale meat costs £70 per pound.

Many animal and environmental groups say that the ban must be maintained. Whales are still in danger because they are also threatened by pollution and loss of habitat and food stocks. There are also moral reasons for stopping the slaughter. There is no humane way to kill a whale, and it may take over an hour for a whale caught by an exploding harpoon to die. Most of all, these beautiful and intelligent animals should be left to live in peace rather than used for human economic gain.

■ *What can you do?*

Support the Whale and Dolphin Conservation Society, Greenpeace or the Environmental Investigation Agency. They can also provide you with more information and have action campaigns you can take part in.

Keep up to date on whale issues by watching the news, reading newspapers or through conservation organisations. If a country continues to catch whales or attempts to reintroduce whaling, you can write and protest to the ambassador of that country at the embassy in London.

Working animals

Animals have contributed power and energy to countless human projects. In India today there are 80 million load-bearing animals such as oxen or elephants. Their power output is equivalent to 30,000 megawatts, or about thirty large power stations. Throughout the world donkeys, mules, asses, oxen, yaks, llamas, reindeer, and horses are the 'beasts of burden'. The work done by them for humans is mostly unacknowledged. Although some individual animals have been loved and respected by their owners, most have been treated as animal slaves and worked to death.

As societies develop and industrialise, more and more jobs are taken over by machines. In Britain today, few horses plough fields or pull carts. Most working animals are dogs. Some of the jobs they tackle are rounding up sheep, guiding the blind and deaf, guarding property and sniffing out drugs at airports and docks. These animal workers are highly trained and highly prized and work in close partnership with their human owners or handlers. Working allows them to use their intelligence and natural behaviour patterns – they are rarely bored, as many pet dogs are.

■ *What can you do?*

The Society for the Protection of Animals Abroad (SPANA) work to improve standards of care for working animals, especially in North Africa, and the World Association for Transport Animal Welfare and Studies (TAWS) aim to promote improved health and welfare for draught and transport animals throughout the world. You can find out more from these organisations and support their work.

In Britain, you can support the Guide Dogs for the Blind Association and the Hearing Dogs for the Deaf organisation.

Zoos

Anti-zoo campaigners say that zoos are cruel prisons where wild animals serve a life sentence. By their very nature zoos mean captivity for wild animals and many zoo animals were, and still are, kept in appalling conditions. In a 1988 survey of European zoos, Zoo Check visited over 1,000 zoos and animal collections and did not class one as 'really good'.

The main criticisms of zoos are that animals live in badly designed enclosures with inadequate space, an unnatural habitat or climate, and an unsuitable diet. They often have no company or breeding groups and nothing to counteract the boredom. These conditions can produce abnormal behaviour such as pacing, swaying, overeating or starving, self-mutilation or abnormal sexual practices.

But there are also convincing arguments in favour of zoos. Zoos can educate the public about wild animals and undertake important research on their behaviour and biology. Zoos may also be vital in conserving ENDANGERED SPECIES. Some zoos have captive breeding programmes with animals being reintroduced to the wild, and some species, such as the Arabian oryx and Hawaiian goose, would be extinct by now without them. Zoos can also provide enjoyable contact between humans and other animals, and for many people living in cities it may be their only chance to see wild animals. This contact may encourage them to support conservation measures and feel a link between themselves and animals.

There is a growing trend for zoos to base their enclosures on the animal's natural behaviour, social groups and habitat. In Glasgow Zoo, for example, animals are kept in social groups wherever possible. They have platforms and structures to climb on, smell trails, and their food is hidden around the enclosure so that they have to find it. This means they spend a lot of the day doing more or less what they would do in the wild. As a result, the animals are less bored and stressed. In other zoos it is the human visitors who are caged. They have to walk through tunnels and walkways within the large enclosures which simulate the animals' natural habitat.

Do we have a right to keep wild animals in captivity? Are there good conservation, research and educational reasons for doing so? Is entertainment and pleasure a good enough reason?

■ What can you do?

Zoo Check is the organisation which aims to prevent abuse to captive animals, phase out zoos, end the taking of animals from the wild and promote the conservation of animals in their natural habitat. You can join them and receive their newsletter.

Think about whether you want to visit a zoo. If you do, and you see examples of cruelty or bad conditions, take photographs and details of the zoo's address and send them to Zoo Check. Because of poor licensing enforcement around the world, there are not accurate records of every zoo. Zoo Check are trying to compile a list of the world's zoos, and ask people on holiday who visit zoos to send them a copy of the zoo guidebook and photographs, if possible.

Directory of organisations

This is an alphabetical list of organisations you can write to for further information, as well as the addresses of bodies such as the House of Commons and European Parliament. Most of the organisations listed are mentioned in the text.

Another good source of useful addresses is *Who's Who in the Environment*, available free from The Environment Council, 80 York Way, London N1 9AG (Tel: 071 278 4736) and *Who's Who in the Environment Scotland*, available free from Countryside Commission for Scotland, Battleby, Redgorton, Perth PH1 3EW (Tel: 0738 27921).

When you write to any organisation, state clearly what you want and remember to include your own name and address. **Also include a stamped and addressed envelope or label**. Many organisations are charities, and are short of funds.

An asterisk* next to the name of an organisation means that it is a group especially for young people.

BRITISH AND INTERNATIONAL ORGANISATIONS

Advertising Standards Authority (ASA)
Brook House, 2–16 Torrington Place, London WC1E 7HN
Tel: 071–580 5555

Advocates for Animals
10 Queensferry Street, Edinburgh EH2 4PG
Tel: 031–2225 6039

Amateur Entomological Society
22 Salisbury Road, Feltham, Middx TW13 5DP
Tel: 081–890 3584

Anglican Society for the Welfare of Animals
10 Chester Avenue, Hawkenbury, Tunbridge Wells, Kent TN2 4TZ
Tel: 0892 25594

Animal Aid
7 Castle Street, Tonbridge, Kent TN9 1BH
Tel: 0732 364546

*Animal Aid Youth Group
7 Castle Street, Tonbridge, Kent TN9 1BH
Tel: 0732 364546

Animal Liberation Front Supporters Group
BCM Box 1160, London WC1N 3XX

Animals Concern (Scotland)
64 Dunbarton Road, Glasgow G3 8RE
Tel: 041–334 6014

*The Animals' Defenders
261 Goldhawk Road, London W12 9PE
Tel: 081–846 9777

Animals in Medicines Research Information Centre (AMRIC)
12 Whitehall, London SW1A 2DY
Tel: 071–588 0841

The Athene Trust
3A Charles Street, Petersfield, Hants GU32 3EH
Tel: 0730 68070

Beauty Without Cruelty Ltd
37 Avebury Avenue, Tonbridge, Kent TN9 1TL
Tel: 0732 365291

The Body Shop International plc
Hawthorn Road, Wick, Littlehampton, West Sussex BN17 7LR
Tel: 0903 717107

British Association for the Advancement of Science
Fortress House, 23 Savile Row, London W1X 1AB
Tel: 071–494 3326

British Association for Shooting and Conservation (BASC)
Marford Mill, Rossett, Clwyd LL12 0HL
Tel: 0244 570881

British Field Sports Society
59 Kennington Road, London SE1 7PZ
Tel: 071–928 4742

British Hedgehog Preservation Society
Knowbury House, Knowbury, Ludlow, Shropshire SY8 3LQ

British Holistic Medicine Association
179 Gloucester Place, London NW1 6DX
Tel: 071–262 5299

British Tarantula Society
81 Phillimore Place, Radlett, Herts WD 8NJ
Tel: 0923 856071

British Union for the Abolition of Vivisection (BUAV)
16a Crane Grove, London N7 8LB
Tel: 071–700 4888

British Veterinary Association
7 Mansfield Street, London W1M 0AT
Tel: 071–636 6541

British Youth Council
57 Chalton St, London NW1 1HU
Tel: 071–387 7559

Broadcasting Standards Council
5–8 The Sanctuary, London SW1P 3JS
Tel: 071–233 0544

Campaign Against Leather and Fur (CALF)
Box 17, 198 Blackstock Rd, London N5 1EN

Campaign for the Abolition of Angling
PO Box 130, Sevenoaks, Kent TN14 5NR

Campaign for Nuclear Disarmament (CND)
162 Holloway Road, London N7 8DQ
Tel: 071–700 2393

Captive Animals Protection Society (CAPS)
36 Braemore Court, Kingsway, Hove, East Sussex BN3 4FG
Tel: 0273 737756

Cat Action Trust (CAT)
PO Box 1639, London W8 4RY

Catholic Study Circle for Animal Welfare
39 Onslow Gardens, South Woodford, London E18 1ND
Tel: 081–989 0478

The Cats Protection League
17 King's Road, Horsham, West Sussex RH13 5PP
Tel: 0403 65566

Chickens' Lib
PO Box 2, Holmfirth, Huddersfield HD7 1QT
Tel: 0484 688650

The Christian Consultative Council for the Welfare of Animals
269 Belstead Road, Ipswich, Suffolk IP2 2DY

Compassion in World Farming
20 Lavant Street, Petersfield, Hants GU32 3EW
Tel: 0730 64208

The Conservative Party
Central Office, 32 Smith Square, London SW1P 3HH
Tel: 071–222 9000

The Cosmetics, Toiletry and Perfumery Association (CTPA)
35 Dover Street, London W1X 3RA
Tel: 071–491 8891

Country Landowners Association
16 Belgrave Square, London SW1X 8PQ
Tel: 071–235 0511

Countryside Council for Wales
Plas Penrhos, Ffordd Penrhos, Bangor, Gwynedd LL57 2LQ
Tel: 0248 370444

Department of the Environment (DoE)
2 Marsham Street, London SW1P 3EB
Tel: 071–276 3000

Department of the Environment – Endangered Species Branch
Tollgate House, Houlton Street, Bristol BS2 9DJ
Tel: 0272 218202

Disabled Against Animal Research and Exploitation
PO Box 8, Daventry, Northants NN11 4RQ

Doctors in Britain Against Animal Experiments (DBAE)
PO Box 302, London N8 9HD

Dolphin Circle
8 Dolby Road, London SW6 3MF
Tel: 071–794 7879 or 071–736 8816

Dr Hadwen Trust for Humane Research
6c Brand Street, Hitchen, Herts SG5 1HX
Tel: 0462 436819

*Earth Action
26–28 Underwood Street, London N1 7JQ
Tel: 071–490 1555

Earthkind
Humane Education Centre, Bounds Green Road, London N22 4EU
Tel: 081–889 1595

Elefriends
Cherry Tree Cottage, Coldharbour, Dorking, Surrey RH5 6HA
Tel: 0306 712091

English Nature
Northminster House, Peterborough PE1 1UA
Tel: 0733 340345

Environmental Investigation Agency (EIA)
208–209 Upper Street, London N1 1RL
Tel: 071–704 9441

EURONICHE (European Network of Individuals and Campaigns
for Humane Education)
c/o Bryony Close, Lankforst 30–31, 6538 JE, Nijmegen, The
Netherlands

European Parliament
97–113 rue Belliard, B–1040 Brussels, Belgium

European Parliament – UK Office
2 Queen Anne's Gate, London SW1H 9AA
Tel: 071–222 0411

European Parliament Information Office
8 Storeys Gate, London SW1P 3AT
Tel: 071–222 8122

Farm Animal Welfare Council
Block C, Government Buildings, Hook Rise South, Tolworth, Surbiton, Surrey KT6 7NF

The Farm and Food Society (FAFS)
4 Willifield Way, London NW11 7XT
Tel: 081–455 0634

*Farm Watch
20 Lavant Street, Petersfield, Hants GU32 3EW
Tel: 0730 64208

Fauna and Flora Preservation Society (FFPS)
1 Kensington Gore, London SW7 2AR
Tel: 071–823 8899

Federation of British Aquatic Societies
10 Rosken Grove, Farnham Royal, Bucks SL2 3DZ
Tel: 0753 645675

Foodline
Food Safety Advisory Centre, 14 Soho Square, London W1V 5FB
Tel: 0800 282407

*Fox Cubs
PO Box 1, Carlton PDO, Nottingham NG4 2JY
Tel: 0602 590357

Free-Range Egg Association (FREGG)
37 Tanza Road, London NW3 2UA
Tel: 071–435 2596

Friends of the Earth (FOE)
26–28 Underwood Street, London N1 7JQ
Tel: 071–490 1555

Friends of the Earth (Scotland)
70–72 New Haven Road, Edinburgh EH6 5QG
Tel: 031–554 9977

Fund for the Replacement of Animals in Medical Experiments (FRAME)
Eastgate House, 34 Stoney Street, Nottingham NG1 1NB
Tel: 0602 584740

Game Conservancy
Burgate Manor, Fordingbridge, Hants SP6 1EF
Tel: 0425 52381

The Genetics Forum
258 Pentonville Road, London N1 9JY
Tel: 071–278 0955

The Green Party
10 Station Parade, Balham High Street, London SW12 9AZ
Tel: 081–673 0045

Greenpeace
Canonbury Villas, Islington, London N1 2RP
Tel: 071–354 5100

Guide Dogs for the Blind Association
Alexandra House, 9 Park Street, Windsor, Berks SL4 1LU
Tel: 0753 855711

Health Education Authority
Hamilton House, Mabledon Place, London WC1H 9TX
Tel: 071–383 3833

Hearing Dogs for the Deaf
The Training Centre, London Road (A40), Lewknor, Oxford OX9 5RY
Tel: 0844 53898

Henry Doubleday Research Association (HDRA)
National Centre for Organic Gardening, Ryton-on-Dunsmore, Coventry CV8 3LG
Tel: 0203 303517

Home Office
50 Queen Anne's Gate, London SW1H 9AT
Tel: 071–273 3000

House of Commons
London SW1A 0AA
Tel: 071–219 3000

Humane Research Trust
Brook House, 29 Bramhall Lane South, Bramhall, Stockport, Cheshire SK7 2DN
Tel: 061–439 8041

Humane Slaughter Association
34 Blanche Lane, South Mimms, Potters Bar, Herts EN6 3PA
Tel: 0707 59040

Hunt Saboteurs Association
PO Box 1, Carlton, Nottingham NG4 2JY
Tel: 0602 590357

Independent Television Commission (ITC)
70 Brompton Road, London SW3 1EY
Tel: 071–584 7011

Institute for Complementary Medicine
21 Portland Place, London W1N 3AF
Tel: 071–636 9543

International Council for Bird Preservation (ICBP)
32 Cambridge Road, Girton, Cambridge CB3 0PJ
Tel: 0223 277318

International Fund for Animal Welfare (IFAW)
Tubwell House, New Road, Crowborough, East Sussex TN6 2HQ
Tel: 08926 63374

International Green Flag
PO Box 396, Linton, Cambridge CB1 6UL

International Jewish Vegetarian Society
855 Finchley Road, London NW11 8LX
Tel: 081–455 0692

International Muslim Association for Animals and Nature (IMAAN)
7 Hurst Road, East Molesey, Surrey KT8 9AQ

International Primate Protection League
116 Judd Street, London WC1H 9NS
Tel: 071–837 7227

International Whaling Commission (IWC)
The Red House, Station Road, Histon, Cambridge CB4 4NP
Tel: 0223 233971

Jockey Club
42 Portman Square, London W1H 0EN
Tel: 071–486 4921

Kennel Club
1–5 Clarges Street, London W1Y 8AB
Tel: 071–493 6651

The Labour Party
150 Walworth Road, London SE17 1JT
Tel: 071–703 0833

League Against Cruel Sports
Sparling House, 83–87 Union Street, London SE1 1SG
Tel: 071–403 6155

The Liberal Democrat Party
4 Cowley Street, London SW1P 3NB
Tel: 071–222 7999

Liberty (National Council for Civil Liberties)
21 Tabard Street, London SE1 4LA
Tel: 071–403 3888

London Food Commission
88 Old Street, London EC1V 9AR
Tel: 071–250 1021

London Zoo Education Department
Regent's Park, London NW1 4RY
Tel: 071–722 3333

The Lord Dowding Fund for Humane Research (LDF)
261 Goldhawk Road, London W12 9PE
Tel: 081–846 9777

Lynx
PO Box 300, Nottingham NG1 5HN
Tel: 0602 413052

Marine Conservation Society (MCS)
9 Gloucester Road, Ross-on-Wye, Herefordshire HR9 5BU
Tel: 0989 66017

Meat and Livestock Commission
PO Box 44, Winterhill House, Snowdon Drive, Milton Keynes MK6 1AX
Tel: 0908 677577

Milk Marketing Board
Giggs Hill Green, Portsmouth Road, Thames Ditton, Surrey KT7 0EL
Tel: 081–398 41014

Ministry of Agriculture, Fisheries and Food (MAFF)
Whitehall Place, London SW1A 4JU
Tel: 071–270 8080

Mocatan
Studio 205, I–Mex Building, Sunbeam Street, Wolverhampton WV2 4NU
Tel: 0902 21421

National Anti-Vivisection Society (NAVS)
261 Goldhawk Road, London W12 9PE
Tel: 081–846 9777

National Canine Defence League
1–2 Pratt Mews, London NW1 0AD
Tel: 071–388 0137

National Centre for Biotechnology Education
Department of Microbiology, University of Reading, Whiteknights, PO Box 228, Reading, Berks RG6 2AJ
Tel: 0734 873743

National Coursing Club (NCC)
16 Clocktower Mews, Newmarket, Suffolk CB8 8LL

National Farmers Union (NFU)
Agriculture House, Knightsbridge, London SW1X 7NJ
Tel: 071–235 5077

National Federation of Anglers (NFA)
Halliday House, 2 Wilson Street, Derby DE1 1PG
Tel: 0332 362000

National Federation of Badger Groups (NFBG)
c/o 16 Ashdown Gardens, Sanderstead, South Croydon, Surrey CR2 9DR
Tel: 081–657 4636

National Petwatch
PO Box 16 Brighouse, West Yorkshire HD6 1DS
Tel: 0484 722411

National Trust
36 Queen Anne's Gate, London SW1H 0AS
Tel: 071–222 9251

National Union of Students (NUS)
461 Holloway Road, London N7 6LJ
Tel: 071–272 8900

Nature Conservancy Council for Scotland
12 Hope Terrace, Edinburgh EH9 2AS
Tel: 031–447 4784

Network of Individuals and Campaigns for Humane Education (NICHE)
c/o Department of Psychology, University of Stirling, Scotland FK5 4LA
Tel: 0786 51324

Nurses' Anti-Vivisectionist Movement
2 Hillcrest Cottage, Hillcrest, Uppertown, Bonsall, Derbyshire DE4 2AW
Tel: 0629 824664

Parents for Safe Food
c/o National Food Alliance, 102 Gloucester Place, London W1H 3DA
Tel: 071–935 2099

People's Dispensary for Sick Animals (PDSA)
Whitechapel Way, Priorslee, Telford, Shropshire TF2 9PQ
Tel: 0952 290999

Quaker Concern for Animals
Webbs Cottage, Woolpits Road, Saling, Braintree, Essex, CM7 5DZ
Tel: 0371 850423

Research Defence Society (RDS)
Grosvenor Gardens House, Grosvenor Gardens, London SW1W 0BS
Tel: 071–828 8745

Royal Entomological Society (RES)
41 Queens Gate, London SW7 5HU
Tel: 071–584 8361

Royal Society for Nature Conservation (RSNC)
The Green, Witham Park, Lincoln LN5 7JR
Tel: 0522 544400

Royal Society for the Prevention of Cruelty to Animals (RSPCA)
Causeway, Horsham, West Sussex RH12 1HG
Tel: 0403 64181

Royal Society for the Protection of Birds (RSPB)
The Lodge, Sandy, Bedfordshire SG19 2DL
Tel: 0767 680551

Scottish National Party (SNP)
6 North Charlotte Street, Edinburgh EH2 4JH
Tel: 031–226 3661

Scottish Society for the Prevention of Cruelty to Animals (SSPCA)
19 Melville Street, Edinburgh EH3 7PL
Tel: 031–225 6418

Society for the Protection of Animals Abroad (SPANA)
15 Buckingham Gate, London SW1E 6LB
Tel: 071–828 0997

Soil Association
86 Colston Street, Bristol BS1 5BB
Tel: 0272 290661

Student Campaign for Animal Rights (SCAR)
Mandela Building, 99 Oxford Road, Manchester

Survival International
310 Edgware Road, London W2 1DY
Tel: 071–723 5535

Teachers for Animal Rights
29 Lynwood Road, London SW17 8SR

Tidy Britain Group
The Pier, Wigan WN3 4EX
Tel: 0942 824620

Trust for the Protection of Reptiles
College Gates, 2 Deansway, Worcester WR1 2JD
Tel: 0483 417550

Universities Federation for Animal Welfare (UFAW)
8 Hamilton Close, South Mimms, Potters Bar, Herts EN6 3QD
Tel: 0707 58202

The Vegan Society
7 Battle Road, St Leonards-on-Sea, East Sussex TN37 7AA
Tel: 0424 427393

The Vegetarian Society
Parkdale, Dunham Road, Altrincham, Cheshire WA14 4QG
Tel: 061–928 0793

*The Vegetarian Society Youth Group
Parkdale, Dunham Road, Altrincham, Cheshire WA14 4QG
Tel: 061–928 0793

Waste Watch
68 Grafton Way, London
Tel: 071–383 3320

*WATCH
The Green, Witham Park, Lincoln LN5 7JR
Tel: 0522 544400

Whale and Dolphin Conservation Society
20 West Lea Road, Bath, Avon BA1 3RL
Tel: 0225 334511

World Association for Transport Animal Welfare and Studies
(TAWS)
c/o Mr G. Hovell, Department of Physiology, Parks Road, Oxford
OX1 3PT
Tel: 0865 272545

World Society for the Protection of Animals (WSPA)
1A Park Place, Lawn Lane, London SW8 1UA
Tel: 071–793 0540

World Wide Fund for Nature – UK (WWF)
Panda House, Weyside Park, Godalming, Surrey GU7 7RX
Tel: 0483 426444

WWF Network on Conservation and Religion
WWF International, Ch–1196 Gland, Switzerland

WWOOF – Working Weekends on Organic Farms
19 Bradford Road, Lewes, East Sussex BN7 1RB

Young Ornithologists' Trust
RSPB, The Lodge, Sandy, Bedfordshire SG19 2DL
Tel: 0767 680551

*Young People's Trust for Endangered Species
95 Woodbridge Road, Guildford, Surrey GU1 4PY
Tel: 0483 39600

*Youth and Education Countryside Trust
Marford Mill, Rossett, Wrexham, Clwyd LL12 0HL
Tel: 0244 570881

Zoo Check
Cherry Tree Cottage, Coldharbour, Dorking, Surrey RH5 6HA
Tel: 0306 712091

AUSTRALIA

Animal Liberation
PO Box 221, Mitcham, Victoria 3132

Australian Association for Humane Research
PO Box 779, Darlinghurst, New South Wales 2010

Australian Biotechnology Association
PO Box 303, Clayton, Victoria 3168

Friends of the Earth
366 Smith Street, Collingwood, Victoria 3066

Project Jonah
672B Glenferrie Road, Hawthorn, Victoria 3122

CANADA

Animal Alliance of Canada
1640 Bayview Avenue, Suite 1916, Toronto, Ontario M4G 4E9

Friends of the Earth
251 Laurier Avenue West, Suite 701, Ottawa, Ontario KIP 5J6

International Fund for Animal Welfare
PO Box 556, Station T, Toronto, Ontario M6B 4C2

Sea Shepherd International
PO Box 48446, Vancouver, BC V7X 1A2

World Society for the Protection of Animals
55 University Avenue, Suite 902, PO Box 15, Toronto, Ontario M5J 2H7

World Wide Fund for Nature
201 St Clair Avenue East, Toronto, Ontario M4T 1NS

NEW ZEALAND

Friends of the Earth
PO Box 39, 065 Auckland West, New Zealand

Society for the Prevention of Cruelty to Animals,
PO Box 43221, Mangere, Auckland

World Wide Fund for Nature
Box 6237, Wellington, New Zealand

SOUTH AFRICA

Dolphin Action and Protection Group
PO Box 2227, Fish Hoek 7975

South African Association Against Painful Experiments on Animals,
PO Box 85228, Emmarentia 2029, Johannesburg

USA

American Anti-Vivisection Society
Suite 204, Noble Plaza, 801 Old York Road, Jenkintown, PA 19046

American Fund for Alternatives to Animal Research, 175 West 12th
Street, Suite 16g, New York 10011

American Humane Association (AHA)
5351 South Raslyn St, Englewood, Colorado 80110, USA

Animal Rights Network
456 Monroe Turnpike, Monroe, CT 06468

Culture and Animals Foundation
3509 Eden Croft Drive, Raleigh, NC 27612

Farm Animal Reform Movement
PO Box 30654, Bethesda, MD 20824

The Humane Society of the United States
2100 L Street, NW Washington, DC 20037

International Fund for Animal Welfare
PO Box 193, Yarmouth Port, MA 02675

Lynx
Suite 155, 10573 West Pico Boulevard, Los Angeles, CA 90064

People for the Ethical Treatment of Animals (PETA)
PO Box 42516, Washington, DC 20015

Whale Protection Fund
Center for Marine Education, 624 9th St, Washington, DC 20001

World Society for the Protection of Animals
PO Box 190, 29 Perkins Street, Boston, MA 02130

If you want to read more

This is only a selection of books on the subject – there are many more. You can get hold of these books from public libraries or, if you want to buy them, from bookshops. Those which have addresses listed are available only by post from the organisation concerned.

GENERAL

The Animal Contract, Dr Desmond Morris.
Virgin, 1990

The Extended Circle, ed. Jon Wynne-Tyson.
Centaur, 1985

Let's Discuss Animal Rights, P. J. Allison.
Wayland, 1986

Pocketbook of Animal Facts and Figures, Barry Kew.
Green Print, 1991

The Use and Abuse of Animals, Zoë Richmond-Watson.
Macdonald Educational, 1984

Voiceless Victims, Rebecca Hall.
Wildwood House, 1984

ANIMAL RIGHTS AND ANIMAL LIBERATION

Animal Liberation, Peter Singer.
Jonathan Cape, 1976

Animal Liberation: A Graphic Guide, Lori Gruen, Peter Singer and David Hine.
Camden Press, 1987

Animal Rights (Points of View Series), Barbara James.
Wayland, 1990

Animal Rights (Survival Series), Miles Barton.
Franklin Watts, 1987

Towards Animal Rights, Animal Aid Report No. 1, Martyn Ford.
Animal Aid, 1984

Why Animal Rights?
Animal Aid, 7 Castle Street, Tonbridge, Kent TN9 1BH, 1988

CIRCUSES

The Rose-tinted Menagerie, William Johnson.
Heretic Books, 1990

CRUELTY-FREE LIVING

The Cruelty-Free Shopper, Lis Howlett.
Bloomsbury, 1989

The Green Consumer Guide, John Elkington and Julia Hailes.
Gollancz, 1988

Herbal Cosmetics, Camilla Hepper.
Thorsons, 1987

The Kind Food Guide, Audrey Eyton.
Penguin, 1991

Living Without Cruelty, Mark Gold.
Green Print, 1988

Natural Beauty, Roy Genders.
Webb & Bower, 1986

The Organic Consumer Guide, ed. David Mabey and Alan and Jackie Gear.
Thorsons, 1990

Save the Animals!, Ingrid Newkirk.
Angus & Robertson, 1991

DISSECTION

Animals in Science Teaching: A Directory of Audio Visual Alternatives
Universities Federation for Animal Welfare, 8 Hamilton Close, South Mimms, Potters Bar, Herts EN6 3QD, 1988

DISSECTION IN SCHOOLS

RSPCA, Purchase and Supply Department, Causeway, Horsham, West Sussex RH12 1HG

ENVIRONMENT

Blueprint for a Green Planet, John Seymour and Herbert Girardet.
Dorling Kindersley, 1987

Ecology, Richard Spurgeon.
Usborne, 1988

The Gaia Atlas of Planet Management, ed. Norman Myers.
Pan, 1985

The Green Consumer Guide, John Elkington and Julia Hailes.
Gollancz, 1988

How to be Green, John Button.
Century Hutchinson, 1989

The Young Person's Guide to Saving the Planet, Debbie Silver and Bernadette Vallely.
Virago, 1990

FARMING

Assault and Battery, Mark Gold.
Pluto, 1983

Chicken and Egg, Clare Duce.
Green Print, 1989

HEALTH

Diary of a Teenage Health Freak, Anne McPherson and Aidan Macfarlane.
Oxford, 1987

Health With Humanity, ed. Steve McIvor.
British Union for the Abolition of Vivisection, 16a Crane Grove, London N7 8LB, 1990

HOLIDAYS

The Good Tourist – A Worldwide Guide for the Green Traveller, Kate Wood and Syd House.
Mandarin, 1991

The 1991 International Vegetarian Travel Guide, ed. Viv Preece.
The Vegetarian Society, Parkdale, Dunham Road, Altrincham, Cheshire WA14 4QG, 1991

HOMES AND GARDENS

Green Living: Practical Ways to Make Your Home Environment Friendly, Bernadette Vallely.
Thorsons, 1991

Home Ecology, Karen Christensen.
Arlington, 1989

Month-by-Month Organic Gardening, Lawrence Hills.
Thorsons, 1989

HUNTING, SHOOTING AND FISHING

Finding Out About Country Sports, Robin Page.
Hobsons, 1989

Hunting, Shooting and Fishing, Philip Neal.
Dryad, 1987

The Tradition of Stag Hunting on Exmoor, Devon and Somerset Residents' Association.
League Against Cruel Sports, Sparling House, 83–87 Union Street, London SE1 1SG

PETS

Catwatching, Desmond Morris.
Jonathan Cape, 1986

Dogwatching, Desmond Morris.
Jonathan Cape, 1986

In the Company of Animals, James Serpell.
Blackwell, 1988

SCHOOL ANIMALS

Animals in Schools Guidelines

Small Mammals in Schools

Both from RSPCA, Purchase and Supply Department, Causeway, Horsham, West Sussex RH12 1HG

TRIBAL PEOPLES

The Gaia Atlas of First Peoples
Robertson-McCarta, 1990

Living Arctic, Hugh Brody.
Faber & Faber, 1987

VEGANISM AND VEGETARIANISM

The Caring Cook: Cruelty-Free Cooking for Beginners, Janet Hunt.

The Vegan Cookbook, Alan Wakeman and Gordon Baskerville.

Why Vegan?, Kath Clements.

All from The Vegan Society, 7 Battle Road, St Leonards-on-Sea, East Sussex TN37 7AA

Sarah Brown's Vegetarian Cookbook, Sarah Brown.
Grafton, 1986

Why You Don't Need Meat, Peter Cox.
Thorsons, 1986

The 1991 International Vegetarian Travel Guide, ed. Viv Preece.
The Vegetarian Society, Parkdale, Dunham Road, Altrincham, Cheshire WA14 4QG

VIVISECTION

The Cruel Deception: The Use of Animals in Medical Research, Dr Robert Sharpe.
Thorsons, 1988

Finding out about Animal Experiments
Hobsons, 1987

The Plague Dogs, Richard Adams (fiction).
Penguin, 1978

What is Vivisection?
British Union for the Abolition of Vivisection, 16a Crane Grove, London N7 8LB

WARFARE

The Military Abuse of Animals
British Union for the Abolition of Vivisection, 16a Crane Grove, London N7 8LB

WILDLIFE

Close to Extinction, J. Burton.
Franklin Watts, 1988

Killing for Luxury, Michael Bright.
Franklin Watts, 1988

Problems with Badgers?
RSPCA, Purchase and Supply Department, Causeway, Horsham,
West Sussex RH12 1HG, 1988

Red Ice: My Fight to Save the Seals, Brian Davies.
Mandarin, 1990

Reptiles: Misunderstood, Mistreated and Mass-marketed
Trust for the Protection of Reptiles, College Gates, 2 Deansway,
Worcester WR1 2JD, 1991

Whale Nation, Heathcote Williams.
Jonathan Cape, 1988

ZOOS

Beyond the Bars: The Zoo Dilemma, ed. Virginia McKenna, Will
Travers and Jonathon Wray.
Thorsons, 1987

The Stationary Ark, Gerald Durrell.
Collins, 1976

Why Zoos?
Universities Federation for Animal Welfare, 8 Hamilton Close,
South Mimms, Potters Bar, Herts EN6 3QD, 1988

Zoo 2000, Jeremy Cherfas.
BBC Books, 1984

Zoos and Game Reserves, Miles Barton.
Franklin Watts, 1988

VIDEOS AND SLIDESETS

The following organisations have videos or slidesets you can hire or buy. The addresses of the organisations are in the directory in this book. You will need to contact them for details of titles and prices.

Animal Aid
The Athene Trust
Beauty Without Cruelty
British Field Sports Society
British Union for the Abolition of Vivisection
Compassion in World Farming
Lynx
National Anti-Vivisection Society
Royal Society for the Prevention of Cruelty to Animals
Scottish Society for the Prevention of Cruelty to Animals
Universities Federation for Animal Welfare
The Vegetarian Society
Zoo Check

Other Virago Upstarts

OUT IN THE OPEN
A Guide for Young People Who Have Been Sexually Abused

Ouainé Bain and Maureen Sanders

'The most surprising thing for me was to find out that it wasn't some weird thing that happened just to me'

If you have ever experienced any kind of sexual abuse, this book is for you. Plain-speaking and sympathetic, it cuts through the terrible loneliness and silence and talks frankly about the range of feelings sexually abused young people experience. Including other people's stories and discussing honestly what can happen once the truth is told, it also offers practical advice and encouragement to young people on the road to recovery. Ultimately this is an optimistic book, arguing and believing that despite the pain, anger, fears and setbacks, once things are out in the open, victims *can* become survivors.

LOVE TALK
A Young Person's Guide To Sex, Love and Life

Eleanor Stephens

With Cartoons by Jonathan Bairstow

A Channel Four Book to tie in with a ten-part TV series

Sex, love and all that stuff can be fun, exciting, enthralling and, for teenagers, a mine-field. Firmly believing that once they have information that is accurate and accessible, young people are capable of handling the powerful changes and important choices that characterise this period, Eleanor Stephens and Jonathan Bairstow have produced an invaluable book to help young people in life and love.

Contents:
Body Talk ● Mind Talk ● Sex Talk ● The First Time Safe Loving ● Birth Control ● Who Am I? ● Coping With Love ● How Do I Look? ● Baby Talk ● Health Check Sex-Related Diseases ● Sex And The Law ● Jealousy ● Friendship

THE YOUNG PERSON'S GUIDE TO SAVING THE PLANET

Debbie Silver and Bernadette Vallely

All you ever wanted to know about the environment but didn't know who to ask, where to look, what to do . . .

Acid rain, batteries, beauty, CFCs, deodorants, E numbers, the greenhouse effect, hamburgers, noise, the ozone layer, rainforests, television, whales . . . over one hundred environmental issues are all here in a simple A-Z format. But that's only the beginning. This book shows you what action *you* can take, ranging from small life changes to ways of encouraging family, friends, schools, supermarkets – even industry and governments – to 'go green'. Saving the planet is a tall order. But it's our only world and our only chance. You could make a difference.

FALLING FOR LOVE
Teenage Mothers Talk

Sue Sharpe

'To start with I felt ashamed of myself really. But after he was born I thought, why should I care what anybody else thinks? It's great to have a baby'

Becoming a mother when you're still a teenager means growing up fast, with not much freedom and a lot of responsibility. But it can add an enormous amount of love and meaning to life. In *Falling for Love*, young mothers give their own stories – telling how boyfriends and parents, schoolfriends and teachers have reacted. They also talk about adoption, living with parents or alone, coping with school or work, and the joys and troubles of having a child when you're still very young. It can happen to anyone, and this sensitive and moving book tells what it's really like.

THE YEAR IT RAINED

Crescent Dragonwagon

'She loves me. Too much. There is nothing I can do to make her happy. Sometimes it seems to me that's all my mother has ever wanted: for me not to be unhappy. I have let her down'

Elizabeth Stein: seventeen, an uneasy survivor of a suicide attempt, a stint in a mental hospital and the daughter of a mother everyone wants. Hiding behind a self-mocking humour, she observes her bewildering family, longs for her lost friend Tabby, slides between two boyfriends and doggedly, unhappily survives. But survival is not about endurance only. Pining inside Elizabeth is a desire to write, a passion poised and waiting for the courage to risk pain – even unhappiness – before it can 'unfurl for flight'.

SPEAKING OUT
Black Girls in Britain

Audrey Osler

'I want my future here in Britain. I consider it to be my country' – Mumtaz

'My ambition, my one great ambition, is to make it known that Black people can get somewhere' – Gillian

'I hope that white people will read this. They'll find out what Asian and Afro-Caribbean girls think and get a trace of what our lives are like' – Nazrah

Teachers and school; friends and boyfriends; parents and families; the community and the wider world all come under lively and passionate scrutiny in this book. Though painfully, angrily aware of racism and sexism, these girls have an optimistic eye for the future and thought-provoking ideas for change now. Surprising, sobering, revealing – nothing is sacred in *Speaking Out*.

TRANSFORMING MOMENTS

Edited by Scarlett MccGwire

'Revelation! It wasn't like a religious experience or anything, significant moments never are. It's that slow dawning of recognition . . .'

Maya Angelou, Melanie McFadyean, Priscilla Presley, Diane Abbott, Eileen Fairweather and Shreela Ghosh, among others, look to their teenage years to find a turning point that altered the course of their lives. What an extraordinary range of stories emerge: first love in a Jewish ghetto; betrayal and expulsion from school; the exhilaration of leaving home; the impact of Jimi Hendrix; teetering on the brink of suicide; refusing to believe the teacher who says university is not for the likes of you. In all our lives are moments or events – dramatic or quiet – that leave us with the certainty that never again will we be quite the same . . .

VOICES FROM HOME
Girls Talk About Their Families

Sue Sharpe

'When I'm older I can be nicer to my parents and do things without having to lie' – Lai

'I remember my dad saying, "Get out of this house, you upset your mum and me so much"' – Ellie

'I always know they'll stick up for me, whatever. It's something I can't describe, the bond in my family' – Gwyn

Voices From Home explodes the myth of the cosy, happy family into a kaleidoscope of changing patterns. Girls describe their life at home – haven or hell, or both. Here closeness and security jostle with violence and abuse. These are real families – some together, some apart – and no matter what shape it takes, for most girls, family life still pivots around a powerful sense of love and loyalty.